The Wedding Officiant's Manual

A Guide to Writing, Planning and Officiating Wedding Ceremonies

Sunny Dawn Johnston

The Wedding Officiant's Manual:

A Guide to Writing, Planning and Officiating Wedding Ceremonies

ISBN-13: 978-0979811937

For permission requests, write to the publisher:

Sunny Dawn Johnston Productions
4640 W. Redfield Rd. Glendale, AZ 85306-5008

DEDICATION

To all of the couples that have invited me to share in one of the most magical moments of their lives...
Thank you, I am truly honored.

CONTENTS

INTRODUCTION

I have written this book as a guide for you. As a non-denominational Minister, I have officiated many wedding ceremonies over the past ten years and have helped many more create their own unique ceremonies. I know how hard it can be to create and organize a ceremony. To know what goes where, get it in the right order and to feel confident in the final product. When I first began officiating weddings I was scared I was going to miss something. I didn't really know what to do and in what order and ... there was nothing out there to tell me how. I just had to jump in and learn. The ceremonies in this book have been collected over the years from a variety of sources. Ceremonies, in general, are a collaborative effort and the ceremonies in this book are no different. Most have been written by me, some parts by the couples themselves, and some by other ministers. My intention in writing this manual is that in sharing what I have learned over the years it will help you, the Officiant, take the guesswork out of creating the ceremonies, and instead offer you a variety of options to make the job graceful and easy.

Enjoy the Journey - Sunny Dawn Johnston

1

ଛୀଓଓ

Who Can Officiate a Wedding & What You Will Need to Perform a Wedding

You Must Be Ordained

If you are not already ordained as a spiritual leader of a religious community, you must become ordained in order to legally conduct a wedding ceremony.

Attend a seminary or religious training institute to become ordained if you will be performing wedding ceremonies as a vocation.

Obtain online ordination credentials if you will be conducting an occasional wedding ceremony for family or friends. Many Internet sites offer online ordination credentials, as well as instructions and training for performing wedding ceremonies.

Have A Letter of Good Standing (If Necessary)

The Letter of Good Standing is the official document that certifies your Ordination within a ministry. The Letter of Good Standing is the official documentation of your Credentials of Ministry. Some states require this, many do not. Check your state laws to be sure.

Have a Copy of Your Ordination License/Credential

The Ordination Credential is acknowledgment of your ordination. It may be a certificate, a license, or some other form of Ministry Identification. Some states require this to be sent in with the license, many do not. Check your state laws to be sure.

Know the State Laws of Where The Marriage Will Be Performed

Each state has specific laws about who can legally conduct a wedding ceremony. If you are not sure of the laws, contact the local county clerk where the wedding will be held. You can also check these two websites to confirm state laws:

http://www.usmarriagelaws.com/search/united_states/officiants_requirements/index.shtml and

http://marriage.about.com/cs/marriagelicenses/a/officiants.htm

Also, ask what you need to do to register in order to perform a legally binding wedding in that state. **State laws differ.**

A Wedding Certificate for You And The Couple to Sign

In most states, the law is that the Officiant is required to sign a marriage license. And in many cases, the Officiant also is responsible for getting the license signed by 2 witnesses and then mailing the license to the proper state officials. Until the court has received the official license, the marriage is not considered legal by state officials.

2

ೞഠೞ

The Phone Rings ...

"Will you Marry Us?"

You have received the phone call. Will you marry us? It is an absolute gift to have the ability to bring people together in marriage & commitment. It truly is one of life's greatest moments for those that are attending as well as for the soon to be married couple. Being an Officiant is also a great opportunity to be of service to couples by guiding them through the process of creating the ceremony that is right for them. It is a great feeling to know that you are helping two people come together and begin their new life as a couple.

Most of the time, the couples you are working with will have no idea how to create a ceremony, and your input is critical. It has been my experience that Officiant's can also become counselors, wedding planners, food blessers, announcers, DJ's and a variety of different titles throughout the engagement period. Of course, all of this is up to you. You have to decide to what degree of support you can offer and make that clear with your couple.

To help you understand the process, I will share with you mine, from the initial phone call to the I do's. During my initial conversation I follow these basic steps:

- ❖ First, I check to see if I am available. I check the date, time and location.
- ❖ I answer their initial questions about the process and my fees.
- ❖ I schedule a time to meet with the couple in person if local or over the phone, if not. During this meeting, we get to know each other. I ask them questions about themselves, their relationship, their beliefs, etc. We then go through the wedding interview questions (see chapter 8).
- ❖ As we go through the wedding interview questions, it brings about questions for the couple that they have not even considered yet, which is good. It puts them in a place to start focusing on some of the ceremony details, not just the venue, food and guest list. I ask them to get to me with any info they did not know at our initial meeting within two weeks or so.
- ❖ At the end of the meeting, I usually schedule another date about three months out from the wedding date, to go over everything. It is at this point that I send them this book, or the ceremonies that are in it and we create some deadlines to complete the rough drafts.

Unless the couple already has a specific ceremony in mind, we usually work with the format presented in this book, as well as the sample ceremonies, and then we add any other readings they would like to include. I explain to the couple that this is their day, and they get to create it in any way that feel right to them. There are only two parts of a ceremony that are required by law; the wedding vows and pronouncement of marriage. The rest is a matter of personal choice. Most of the couples I work with really have no idea how to create their ceremony. That is why I have created this book. It is intended for you to be able to offer them as many different ideas as possible.

I typically like to have the ceremony completed about two months before the wedding date. If it gets too close to the date, the couple are stressed out and not as present to complete the most important piece of the wedding, the ceremony. I typically do the drafts of the ceremony through email with the couple, and upon completion, I send them a final copy, for approval.

Once the ceremony is written the next step is the rehearsal dinner, if requested. I prefer to have a rehearsal, and it is traditionally held the night before the ceremony, although it can be done a couple hours before the ceremony, if it is a small intimate group. This is the time to meet with everyone, make sure that everyone is on the same page about what has to be done, when, where, and by whom during the ceremony. I like to have everyone walk through the entire ceremony, from beginning to end, so that it calms the nerves and everyone has a feel for what to do. Sometimes, I will have them walk through it two or three times, depending on the ceremony and the wedding party. I find it puts everyone at ease when they know what to do. And, we want everyone at ease, especially the bride and groom.

3

ೞಞ

Wedding Interview Questions

On the following pages you will find a wedding ceremony information sheet to fill out with the bride and groom. This sheet can be used to obtain information about their wedding and the type of ceremony they would like to have as well as help them answer questions they didn't even know they had. You may also access and download the form on my website:

http://sunnydawnjohnston.com/wedding/ SDJ_WeddingInterviewQuestions.pdf

Wedding Ceremony Information Sheet

Date of Ceremony:	Time:	
Date of Rehearsal:	Time:	
Location of Ceremony:		
The Bride/Partner		
Full Name: (No Initials Please):		
Mailing Address:	Phone Number:	
Occupation:	Email Address:	
Full Name of Father:	Living	Deceased
Full Maiden Name of Mother:	Living	Deceased
This is your (1st, 2nd, etc...) marriage	You are: Single Divorced	Widowed
If Divorced, Date of Decree:	State of Issue:	
The Groom/Partner		
Full Name: (No Initials Please):		
Mailing Address:	Phone Number:	
Occupation:	Email Address:	
Full Name of Father:	Living	Deceased
Full Maiden Name of Mother:	Living	Deceased
This is your (1st, 2nd, etc...) marriage	You are: Single Divorced	Widowed

If Divorced, Date of Decree:	State of Issue:
Name of Bride/First Partner to be used in Ceremony:	
Name of Groom/Second Partner to be used in Ceremony:	
Other Important Information:	

The Couple:

1. Have you reviewed the marriage laws for your state?

2. What is the exact location of the wedding?

3. What is the time and date of the ceremony?

Rehearsal:

1. What time do you wish the rehearsal to begin? (Count on it lasting at least one hour)

2. What is the time and location of rehearsal dinner?

3. Do you want the Officiant and Spouse at the rehearsal dinner?

Remind Bride and Groom to bring the license with them to the rehearsal dinner.

Ceremony:

1. What time are pictures?

2. How many guests are expected?

3.   Do you want to include the children, if any?
4.   What names are to be used in Ceremony? (Full Names)
5.   Placement during the Ceremony?
6.   What will the music be? Entrance: Exit:
7.   Will this be a double ring Ceremony? (Not all men choose to wear a ring)
8.   Have you selected vows or do you want me to write some for you?
9.   Who is giving away the Bride?
10.Is there a certain scripture you want to be read?
11.Go over the processional. How is everyone entering?
12.Will you light a Unity Candle? Unity Sand? Placement of the table?

23. What are the wedding colors?

24. Date to have ceremony ideas together by? (Usually about 3 months ahead is best; it gets hectic otherwise)

Thank you for taking the time to complete this form. This will help me serve you both in creating the perfect ceremony for you.

4

ೞೲ

Obtaining a Marriage License

Your bride/groom may obtain a marriage license and apply for a certified copy of the marriage license at the City Clerk of the Courts Customer Service Center in their city/state.

MARRIAGE LICENSE APPLICATION INSTRUCTIONS

The bride and groom will be required to provide a government issued photo I.D. such as a driver's license to show proof of age and confirm identity. Both parties must be present to obtain a marriage license. All state laws are different in regard to what is needed and the amount of time in advance they must receive their marriage license. You are responsible for researching this and giving you client the correct information for their city/state. A copy of a divorce decree may be required as well as a blood test. Check your local city/state laws for more information.

MARRIAGE LICENSE APPLICATION FEE

The fee for a marriage license varies from state to state. Check your local city/state laws for more information.

MARRIAGE LICENSE AGE REQUIREMENTS

In general, if you are under the age of 18, you must either have a notarized parental consent form or have your parent(s) accompany you, present the proper identification, and sign the parental consent form in front of the clerk issuing your license. Check your local city/state laws for more information.

5

ೞುಞ

MOST Marriage Ceremonies Include …

Breakdown of a Typical Non-Denominational

Wedding Ceremony

1. Wedding processional - Entrance of the Bride and Groom and wedding party
2. Opening words by Officiant
3. The giving in marriage
4. Opening prayer, reading, music, literature, or poetry
5. Wedding vows
6. Second reading, music, literature, or poetry
7. Exchange of wedding rings and/or gifts
8. A Unity Ceremony
9. Closing
10. Sanction/Pronouncement of marriage
11. A first kiss as a married couple
12. Introduction as Mr. and Mrs.

13. Wedding Recessional

14. Signing of the wedding certificate or marriage license

Most ceremonies have a combination of the previous fourteen items. The couple can always choose to add or subtract, but this is the basic foundation of a marriage ceremony. Remember, the only two legal requirements are the wedding vows and the sanction of the marriage. The rest is up to them. Your job is to help them understand the purpose of each part of the ceremony and the custom design it with them.

PROCESSIONAL

The Bride traditionally stands to the left of the Groom. So Bride on the left and Groom on the right. This dates back to medieval times when the Groom might need to defend his Bride in the middle of the ceremony, and wanted to leave his right hand, his sword hand, free. The tradition has continued, likely because no one has given it much thought. So, if you feel guided to change it up, feel free. Just know that if you are doing a traditional church ceremony, you may need to follow tradition, so check to be sure.

OPENING WORDS BY OFFICIANT

The wedding begins by welcoming the guests. A traditional and nontraditional example are:

Traditional: *Dearly Beloved, we are gathered here today in the presence of these witnesses, to join {Bride} & {Groom} in matrimony, which is commended to be honorable among all men; and therefore – is not by any – to be entered into unadvisedly or lightly – but reverently, discreetly, advisedly and solemnly. Into this holy state these two persons present now come to be joined. If any person can show just cause why they may not be joined together – let them speak now or forever hold their peace.*

Nontraditional: *Friends, we have been invited here today to share with {Bride}*

& {Groom} a very important moment in their lives. In the years they have been together, their love and understanding of each other has grown and matured, and now they have decided to live their lives together as husband and wife.

THE GIVING IN MARRIAGE

The traditional wording is: "Who gives this woman to be wedded to this man?" The more nontraditional approach, which many couple choose is "Who supports this woman in her marriage to this man?" Many couples chose to skip this part altogether.

OPENING PRAYER, READING OR SONG

This will generally set the tone of your wedding. It could be serious, humorous, sentimental, or elegant. Typically, it says something about love, relationships, or marriages. Some people choose all three, a prayer a reading and a song. Remember, it is their wedding.

> **Prayer:** Heavenly Father, {*Bride*} and {*Groom*} are now about to vow their unending loyalty to each other. We ask you to accept the shared treasure of their life together, which they now create and offer to You. Grant them everything they need, that they may increase in their knowledge of You throughout their life together. In the name of Jesus Christ. Amen.

> **Reading:"To Be One With Each Other" by George Eliot**
> What greater thing is there for two human souls
> than to feel that they are joined together to strengthen
> each other in all labor, to minister to each other in all sorrow,
> to share with each other in all gladness,
> to be one with each other in the
> silent unspoken memories?

> **Song: Norah Jones's "Come Away with Me"?**

WEDDING VOWS

{*name*}, with all my love, I take you to be my wife/husband. I will love you through good and the bad, through joy and the sorrow. I will try to be understanding, and to trust in you completely. Together we will face all of life's experiences and share one another's dreams and goals. I promise I will be your equal partner in a loving, honest relationship, for as long as we both shall live.

SECOND READING OR SONG

"An Irish Wedding Blessing"

You are the star of each night,
You are the brightness of every morning,
You are the story of each guest,
You are the report of every land.
No evil shall befall you, on hill nor bank,
In field or valley, on mountain or in glen.
Neither above, nor below, neither in sea,
Nor on shore, in skies above,
Nor in the depths.
You are the kernel of my heart,
You are the face of my sun,
You are the harp of my music,
You are the crown of my company

EXCHANGE OF RINGS OR GIFTS

The Bride and Groom say something like "I, {name}, give you, {name}, this ring as an eternal symbol of my love and commitment to you."
Or: "I give you this ring to wear with love and joy. As a ring has no end, neither shall my love for you. I choose you to be my (wife / husband) this day and forevermore."

UNITY CEREMONY

Many couples are choosing to add a unity ceremony. They may

choose to do this in silence, with music playing or they may create vows to say about the joining of their families.

The Unity Candle: One of the most common ceremonies. The Bride and Groom each take a lit candle and simultaneously light a third larger "Unity Candle." They may blow out their individual lights, or leave them lit, symbolizing that they have not lost their individuality in their unity.

Variations: All guests are given a candle, and the first guest's is lit. Guests pass the flame until all are lit, and then the Bride and Groom together light their unity candle. Another variation is the mothers or the parents light the first candles and then the Bride and Groom together light their unity candle.

CLOSING

This could be a prayer, scripture, poem or just the sanctioning of the marriage. It is generally the "final thoughts" of the Officiant.

PRAYER: Join with me as we ask God's blessing on this new couple. Eternal Father, Redeemer, we now turn to you; and as the first act of this couple in their newly formed union, we ask you to protect their home. May they always turn to you for guidance, for strength, for provision and direction. May they glorify you in the choices they make, in the ministries they involve themselves in, and in all that they do. Use them to draw others to yourself, and let them stand as a testimony to the world of your faithfulness. We ask this in Jesus' name, Amen.

Scripture: 1 Corinthians chapter 13: verses 4-7

Love is patient, love is kind. It does not envy, it does not boast, it is not proud.

It is not rude, it is not self-seeking, it is not easily angered, it keeps no record of wrongs.

Love does not delight in evil, but rejoices with the truth.

It always protects, always trusts, always hopes, always preservers.

SANCTION/PRONOUNCEMENT OF MARRIAGE

The Officiant typically says something like "By the power vested in me by the State of _____, I now pronounce you husband and wife" or for same-sex couples, "I now pronounce you married."

KISS

The Officiant will usually say something like, "You may now kiss." Or "You may now kiss your bride." Or the Officiant can skip the permission giving, and the couple can just kiss.

INTRODUCTION OF NEWLYWEDS

The Officiant says "I am honored to present to you Mr. and Mrs. _____." Or "I present to you the newly married couple, {*Bride*} & {*Groom*}" if they are not changing their names. The guests stand and applaud, as the couple then leads the recessional out.

RECESSIONAL

The Bride & Groom followed by the wedding party followed by you, the Officiant make your exit .

SIGNING OF THE LICENSE

You sign the marriage license after dinner or snacks but before the cake. I like to sign on the cake table if possible, so that it is pretty. get the photographer to take a few pictures. You will need to gather the best man and maid of honor, or two witnesses in order to sign the license. Congratulations, you have just performed a wedding. Make a copy of the license, once signed, and then send in the next day. Do it for them, so they don't have to worry about it.

6

ೞೞ

Samples of Wedding Ceremonies

Ceremony 1 – Prayer, Scripture and Unity Sand

Best Man: A
B
C

Maid of Honor: A
B
C

OFFICIANT, Groom, and Best Man C already at front.
Best Man A will walk Mother of Bride and Groom to their seats.

(Start playing song on guitar)
Best Man A and Maid of Honor A walk down isle.
Best Man B with Maid of Honor B and C walk down isle.
Ring Boy walks down.
Flower Girl walks down.

(Plays chorus)

Father of the Bride and Bride walk down.
OFFICIANT: Who gives {*Bride*} to be married to {*Groom*}?

Father of the Bride: Her mother and I do.

OFFICIANT: You may be seated! Thank you all for being here today to share in this special ceremony for {*Groom*} and {*Bride*}.

I'd like to begin with Scripture, **"1 Corinthians chapter 13: verses 4-7"**

> 4: Love is patient, love is kind. It does not envy, it does not boast, it is not proud.
> 5: It is not rude, it is not self-seeking, it is not easily angered, it keeps no record of wrongs.
> 6: Love does not delight in evil, but rejoices with the truth.
> 7: It always protects, always trusts, always hopes, always preservers.

OFFICIANT: {*Groom*}, {*Bride*}, It is one of life's greatest gifts when two souls meet and love leads them to proceed together along a path of marriage. It is truly one of life's finest experiences. All of us gathering here today give witness to the love and commitment you are about to express as you take the next step into the journey of husband and wife.

It is important for all of us here today to support {*Groom*} and {*Bride*} and for them to feel the love we hold for them today. Let us all unite and make this the day of their dreams.

Marriage is a commitment to life- to the best that two people can find and bring out in each other. It offers opportunities for sharing and growth no other human relationship can equal, a physical and emotional joining that is promised for a lifetime.

Marriage understands and forgives the mistakes life is unable to avoid. It encourages and nurtures new life, new experiences, and new ways of expressing love through the seasons of life.

When two people pledge to love and care for each other in marriage, they create a spirit unique to themselves, which binds them closer than any spoken or written words. Marriage is a promise, a potential, made in the hearts of two people who love, which takes a lifetime to fulfill.

OFFICIANT: {*Bride*}, do you take this man to be your husband; will you love him, comfort him, honor him, and keep him in sickness and in health; and forsaking all others, be faithful to him as long as you both shall live?

Bride: I do.

OFFICIANT: {*Groom*}, do you take this woman to be your wife; will you love her, comfort her, honor her, and keep her in sickness and in health; and forsaking all others, be faithful to her as long as you both shall live?

Groom: I do.

OFFICIANT: Please bow your head for **PRAYER**
God bless these hands. May they always be held by one another. Give them strength to hold on during the bad times. Keep them tender and gentle. May {*Groom*} and {*Bride*} see their four hands as healer, protector, shelter, and guide. Amen.

VOWS
OFFICIANT: {*Bride*}, please hold hands and repeat after me:

Bride: I, {*Bride*}, take you, {*Groom*}, to be my husband, my partner, my friend, my confidant and my soul mate.

OFFICIANT: {*Groom*}, please repeat after me.

Groom: I, {*Groom*}, take you, {*Bride*}, to be my wife, my partner, my friend, my confidant and my soul mate.

OFFICIANT: May I have the rings please? As you offer these rings, it is a token of your love and devotion for each other. May these rings be blessed as a symbol of this affectionate unity. Your two lives are being joined today in one unbroken circle. Wherever you go, may you always return to one another in your togetherness. May you find in one another the love for which all men and women yearn. May you grow in understanding and compassion. May these rings symbolize the touch of the spirit of love that is in both your hearts.

OFFICIANT: {*Bride*}, please repeat after me:

Bride: {*Groom*}, I give you this ring as a symbol of my love, and with all that I am and all that I have, I pledge my faithful love. May it be a reminder to you that I hold your heart in my care all the days of my life.

OFFICIANT: {*Groom*}, please repeat after me:

Groom: {*Bride*}, I give you this ring as a symbol of my love, and with all that I am and all that I have, I pledge my faithful love. May it be a reminder to you that I hold your heart in my care all the days of my life.

OFFICIANT: This wedding is a uniting of two individual souls into one and yet still retaining their own identity. In joining together with the Unity Sand it is to also represent the two families of this loving couple. It symbolizes that these families have become as one, to show love, acceptance, and support for these two people in their life together. I'd now like to invite {*Groom*}'s parents and {*Bride*}'s parents to come up and join {*Groom*} and {*Bride*} to combine their sand, representing the sands of time and symbolizing the merging of their individual lives and families coming together as one.

OFFICIANT says as they pour: "Today, {*Groom*} and {*Bride*} have chosen to commemorate their marriage through the celebration of the Sand Ceremony. This ceremony symbolizes the inseparable union of {*Groom*} and {*Bride*} into a new and eternal marital relationship. {*Groom*} and {*Bride*} will simultaneously pour separate containers of sand into a common vessel. Each grain of sand in their separate containers represents a unique and separate moment, decision, feeling or event that helped shaped {*Groom*} and {*Bride*} into the separate and unique individuals that they are today. As they pour their separate containers of sand into a common vessel, those separate and independent individuals will merge into a loving and supportive marriage. {*Groom*} and {*Bride*}, just as the grains of sand can never be separated into their individual containers, so are you, together forever."

OFFICIANT: Now that {*Groom*} and {*Bride*} have given themselves to each other by solemn vows, with the joining of hands and the giving and receiving of a ring, it is my privilege as an ordained minister to pronounce that you are husband and wife.

You may now kiss the Bride!

It gives me great pleasure to introduce to you for the first time as husband and wife, Mr. & Mrs. _____!!

BLESSING ON THE FOOD
We give thanks today to God and the Angels for our lives and this beautiful summer day. We thank you for this circle of friends &

family and for the opportunity to be together on this very special occasion. We thank you for reminding us, through {*Groom*} and {*Bride*}, of the true essence and joy of unconditional love.

We give thanks for good food and those who prepare it, for good friends with whom to share it, and for the love which {*Groom*} and {*Bride*} have for each other, we thank you …. Amen.

Ceremony 2 – Child & Unity Sand

OFFICIANT: You may be seated! {*Groom*} & {*Bride*} have asked you all here today to witness the giving and receiving of their wedding vows.

OFFICIANT: Who gives {*Bride*} to be married to {*Groom*}?

Bride's Parents: We do.

OFFICIANT: Marriage is a union, and not always just a union of two. Tonight, not only do {*Groom*} and {*Bride*} become husband and wife, but they become a family. It is a special man that takes on the role of father figure… {*Groom*} and {*Child*} have a unique opportunity to come together and connect as a family with the most important woman in their life. So, let us all unite in making this day a special and memorable day for the soon to be {*Last Name*} family.

OFFICIANT: It is one of life's greatest things when three souls meet and lead them to proceed together along a path of marriage. It is indeed one of life's finest experiences. All of us gathering here give witness to the love and commitment they are about to express. As they take their next step into the journey of husband, wife and child… or family, as we lovingly call it! It is important for all of us here today to support them and for them to feel the love we hold for them today. Let us all unite and make this the day of their dreams.

The little things are the big things.
It is never being too old to hold hands.
It is remembering to say "I love you" at least once a day.
It is never going to sleep angry.
It is at no time taking the other for granted.
The courtship should not end with the honeymoon.
It should continue through all the years.
It is having a mutual sense of values and common objectives.
It is standing together facing the world.
It is forming a circle of love that gathers in the whole family.
It is doing things for each other, not in the attitude of duty or sacrifice; but in the spirit of joy.
It is speaking words of appreciation and demonstrating gratitude in thoughtful ways.
It is not expecting too much from one another.
It is always seeing the good in each other.
It is cultivating flexibility, patience, understanding, and a sense of humor.
It is having the capacity to forgive and forget.
It is giving each other an atmosphere in which each can grow.
It is finding room for the things of the spirit.
It is a common search for the good and the beautiful.
It is establishing a relationship in which the independence is equal; dependence is mutual and the obligation is reciprocal.
It is not only marrying the right partner; it is being the right partner.
Marriage is more than a contract. It is a commitment to take joy deep into the discovery of who you most truly are. It is a commitment to a spiritual journey, to a life of becoming.
Marriage is a covenant that says:

I love you;

I trust you;

I will be here for you when you are hurting;

And when I am hurting I will not leave.

It is not a place where we run from pain, anger or sorrow, but rather a safe sanctuary to risk loving, to risk living, and sharing from the center of oneself.

Let us now bow our heads in prayer:

We Give thanks to God for our lives on this beautiful day. We thank you for this circle of friends and family and for the opportunity to be together on this very special day. We thank you for reminding us, through {*Groom*}, {*Bride*} & {*Child*}, the true essence and joy of unconditional love. Amen.

{*Groom*}, the woman & child standing by your side are about to become your family. They will look to you for gentleness, for support, for understanding, for encouragement, and for protection. You must never take {*Bride*} or {*Child*} for granted, and be continually sensitive to their needs. Your life and love will be their greatest source of joy.

So I ask you, {*Groom*}, will you have {*Bride*} to be your lawfully wedded wife? Will you love and cherish her? Will you always uphold her and encourage here? Will you be loyal to her and true? Will you honor her all her days and be respectful of her, and promise to always bestow upon her your heart's deepest devotion?

Groom: I will.

OFFICIANT: {*Bride*}, the man standing by your side is about to become your husband. He will look to you for gentleness, for support, for understanding, for encouragement, and for protection. You must never take {*Groom*} for granted, and be continually sensitive to his needs. Your life and love will be {*Groom*}'s greatest source of joy.

So I ask you, {*Bride*}, will you have {*Groom*} to be your lawfully wedded husband? Will you love and cherish him? Will you always uphold him and encourage him? Will you be loyal to him and true? Will you honor him all his days and be respectful of him, and promise to always bestow upon him your heart's deepest devotion?

Bride: I will.

OFFICIANT: {*Groom*}, please hold {*Bride*}'s hand.

These are the hands of your best friend. These are the hands the will passionately love you and cherish you through the years, for a lifetime of happiness. These are the hands that will hold you tight as you struggle through difficult times. These are the hands that will comfort you when you are sick, or console you when you are grieving. These are the hands that will hold you in joy and excitement and hope. These are the hands that will give you support as she encourages you to chase down your dreams. Together as a team, everything you wish for can be realized.

OFFICIANT: May I have the rings please? As you offer these rings, it is a token of your love and devotion for each other. May these rings be blessed as a symbol of this affectionate unity. Your lives are being joined today in one unbroken circle. Wherever you go, may you always return to one another in your togetherness. May you find in one another the love for which all men and women yearn. May you grow in understanding and compassion. May these rings symbolize the touch of the spirit of love that is in both your hearts.

(**They will read their vows to each other**)

{*Groom*}, please go ahead and share your vows with {*Bride*}.

Groom: {*Bride*}, this ring I give you today is no ordinary ring. It has very special meaning. It has a heart, to represent the love I have for you. It has hands that represent the friendship I share with you and a crown that reminds you that I am loyal to you. It also has a Celtic heart knot representing the eternal life journey I will share with you. I promise to be by your side, for better or worse, for as long as I shall live.

OFFICIANT: {*Bride*}, please share your vows with {*Groom*}

Bride: {*Groom*}, this ring I give you today is no ordinary ring. It has very special meaning. It has a heart, to represent the love I have for you. It has hands that represent the friendship I share with you and a crown that reminds you that I am loyal to you. It also has a Celtic heart knot representing the eternal life journey I will share with you. I promise to be by your side, for better or worse, for as long as I shall live.

OFFICIANT: {*Groom*}, please place the ring on {*Bride*}'s finger and repeat after me:
I give you this ring as a symbol of my love, and with all that I am, and all that I have, I pledge to you my faithful love.

OFFICIANT: {*Bride*}, please place the ring on {*Groom*}'s finger and repeat after me:
I give you this ring as a symbol of my love, and with all that I am, and all that I have, I pledge to you my faithful love.

OFFICIANT: Read **"Marriage is a Promise" poem**

OFFICIANT: This wedding is a uniting of three individual souls into one and yet still retaining their own identity. In joining together with the Unity Sand, it is to also represent the two families of this loving couple. It symbolizes that these families have become as one, to show love, acceptance, and support for these three people in their life together. I'd now like to invite {*Groom*}'s parents and {*Bride*}'s parents and {*Child*}'s aunt to come up and start the combining of the sand.

Thank you and you may be seated.

Now I'll ask {*Groom*}, {*Bride*} and {*Child*} to now combine their sand, representing the sands of time and symbolizing the merging of their individual lives and families coming together as one.

OFFICIANT: Now that {*Groom*} & {*Bride*} have given themselves to each other by solemn vows, with the joining of hands and the giving and receiving of a ring, it is my privilege as an ordained minister to pronounce you husband and wife.

You may now kiss the Bride!

It gives me great pleasure to introduce to you for the first time together: {*Groom*}, {*Bride*} and {*Child*}.

Ceremony 3 – Traditional Ceremony

OFFICIANT: You may be seated! Thank you all for being here today to share in this special ceremony for {*Groom*} and {*Bride*}.

OFFICIANT: Who gives {*Bride*} to be married to {*Groom*}?

Father of the Bride: Her mother and I do.

Opening Prayer
OFFICIANT: Heavenly Father, {*Bride*} and {*Groom*} are now about to vow their unending loyalty to each other. We ask you to accept the shared treasure of their life together, which they now create and offer

to You. Grant them everything they need, that they may increase in their knowledge of You throughout their life together. In the name of Jesus. Amen.

OFFICIANT: It is one of life's greatest things when two souls meet and lead them to proceed together along a path of marriage. It is indeed one of life's finest experiences. All of us gathering here give witness to the love and commitment they are about to express. As they take their next step into the journey of husband and wife, it is important for all of us here today to support them and for them to feel the love we hold for them today. Let us all unite and make this the day of their dreams.

"Blessing for a Marriage" by James Dillet Freeman

> May your marriage bring all the exquisite excitements
> A marriage should bring,
> And may life grant you also patience, tolerance, and understanding.
> May you always need one another-
> Not so much to fill your emptiness as to help you to know your fullness.
> A mountain needs a valley to be complete:
> The valley does not make the mountain less, but more;
> And the valley is more a valley because it has a mountain towering over it.
> So let it be with you and you.
> May you need one another, but not out of weakness.
> May you want one another, but not out of lack.
> May you entice one another, but not compel one another.
> May you embrace one another, but not encircle one another.
> May you succeed in all important ways with one another,
> And not fail in the little graces.
> May you look for thing to praise, often say, "I love you!"
> And take no notice of small faults.

If you have quarrels that push you apart,
May both of you hope to have good sense enough to take the first step back.
May you enter into the mystery which is the awareness of
One another's presence-
No more physical than spiritual, warm and near when you are side by side,
And warm and near when you are in separate rooms or even distant cities.
May you have happiness, and may you find it making one another happy.
May you have love, and may you find it loving one another!

Thank you, God,
For Your presence here with us
And Your blessings on this marriage.
Amen

OFFICIANT: {*Groom*}, the woman standing by your side is about to become your wife. She will look to you for gentleness, for support, for understanding, for encouragement, and for protection. You must never take {*Bride*} for granted, and be continually sensitive to her needs. Your life and love will be {*Bride*}'s greatest source of joy.

So I ask you, {*Groom*}, will you have {*Bride*} to be your lawfully wedded wife? Will you love and cherish her? Will you always uphold her and encourage here? Will you be loyal to her and true? Will you honor her all her days and be respectful of her, and promise to always bestow upon her your heart's deepest devotion?

Groom: I will.

OFFICIANT: {*Bride*}, the man standing by your side is about to become your husband. He will look to you for gentleness, for support, for understanding, for encouragement, and for protection. You must never take {*Groom*} for granted, and be continually sensitive to his needs. Your life and love will be {*Groom*}'s greatest source of joy.

So I ask you, {*Bride*}, will you have {*Groom*} to be your lawfully wedded husband? Will you love and cherish him? Will you always uphold him and encourage him? Will you be loyal to him and true? Will you honor him all his days and be respectful of him, and promise to always bestow upon him your heart's deepest devotion?

Bride: I will.

OFFICIANT: {*Groom*}, please hold {*Bride*}'s hand.
These are the hands of your best friend. These are the hands the will passionately love you and cherish you through the years, for a lifetime of happiness. These are the hands that will hold you tight as you struggle through difficult times. These are the hands that will comfort you when you are sick, or console you when you are grieving. These are the hands that will hold you in joy and excitement and hope. These are the hands that will give you support as she encourages you to chase down your dreams. Together as a team, everything you wish for can be realized.

{*Groom*}, please repeat after me:
Today before God and all these witnesses, I {*Groom*}, take you, {*Bride*}, to be my wife. To laugh with you in joy, to grieve with you in sorrow, to grow with you in love, to bring you peace and nurture your spirit.

OFFICIANT: {*Bride*}, as you face {*Groom*}:
These are the hands of your best friend, strong and vibrant with love; holding your hand on your wedding day, as he promises to love you all the days of his life. These are the hands that will work alongside

yours, as together you build your future, as you laugh and cry, as you share your innermost secrets and dreams. These are the hands that will love you and cherish you through the years for a lifetime of happiness. These are the hands that will countless times wipe the tears from your eyes – tears of sorrow and tears of joy. These are the hands that will comfort you in illness and hold you when you are frightened or grieving. These are the hands that will tenderly lift your chin and brush your cheek as they raise your face to look into your eyes – eyes that are filled completely with his overwhelming love and desire for you.

{*Bride*}, please repeat after me:
Today before God and all these witnesses, I, {*Bride*}, take you, {*Groom*}, to be my husband. To laugh with you in joy, to grieve with you in sorrow, to grow with you in love, to bring you peace and nurture your spirit.

OFFICIANT: God bless these hands. May they always be held by one another. Give them strength to hold on during the bad times. Keep them tender and gentle. May {*Groom*} and {*Bride*} see their four hands as healing, protection, shelter, and guidance. Amen.

OFFICIANT: May I have the rings please? As you offer these rings, it is a token of your love and devotion for each other. May these rings be blessed as a symbol of this affectionate unity. Your two lives are being joined today in one unbroken circle. Wherever you go, may you always return to one another in your togetherness. May you find in one another the love for which all men and women yearn. May you grow in understanding and compassion. May these rings symbolize the touch of the spirit of love that is in both your hearts.

OFFICIANT: {*Groom*}, please repeat after me:
{*Bride*}, I give you this ring as a symbol of my love, and with all that I am and all that I have, I pledge my faithful love. May it be a reminder

to you that I hold your heart in my care all the days of my life.

OFFICIANT: {*Bride*}, please repeat after me:
{*Groom*}, I give you this ring as a symbol of my love, and with all that I am and all that I have, I pledge my faithful love. May it be a reminder to you that I hold your heart in my care all the days of my life.

Closing Prayer
OFFICIANT: Join with me as we ask God's blessing on this new couple.
Eternal Father, Redeemer, we now turn to you, and as the first act of this couple in their newly formed union, we ask you to protect their home. May they always turn to you for guidance, for strength, for provision and direction. May they glorify you in the choices they make, in the ministries they involve themselves in, and in all that they do. Use them to draw others to yourself, and let them stand as a testimony to the world of your faithfulness. We ask this in Jesus' name, Amen.

OFFICIANT: Now that {*Groom*} and {*Bride*} have given themselves to each other by solemn vows, with the joining of hands and the giving and receiving of a ring, it is my privilege as an ordained minister to pronounce that you are husband and wife.

You may now kiss the Bride!

It gives me great pleasure to introduce to you for the first time as husband and wife, Mr. & Mrs. _____!!

Ceremony 4 – Hand Blessing and Recommitment theme

OFFICIANT: Thank you for being here today to share in this special ceremony for {*Bride*} and {*Groom*}

All of us gathering here this beautiful February evening give witness to the love and commitment they are about to express as they take their next step into the journey of husband and wife.

Life is a story that endlessly unfolds – today we have gathered as {*Bride*} & {*Groom*} choose to join their stories and create a new chapter. It is one of life's greatest blessings when two souls meet and lead them along a path of marriage, a union of trust and the responsibility of being a living example to others of what unconditional love looks like. It is indeed one of life's finest experiences. Their story begins unlike many others. One soul looking for a home, and another soul having a home that feels empty without a life partner. A place to feel comforted, supported and accepted; a sacred place to bring others who are weary with life to surround them with unconditional love, a sanctuary for the tired and the hungry, filled with love and understanding.

Yet, life is filled with uncertainty. The search for security and unconditional love almost seems an illusion. Stepping in to the uncertainty of life is fertile ground of pure creativity and freedom. Uncertainty means stepping into the unknown in every moment of our existence. The unknown is the infinite field of all possibilities, ever fresh, ever new, always open to the creation of new manifestations. This means that in every moment in your life, you will have excitement, adventure and mystery. You will experience the fun of life – the magic, the celebration, the exhilaration, the exultation of your own spirit. Before you today are two loving souls who are willing to step into a world of uncertainty…together, to show up in service of each other and all who come in contact with them.

Everyone plays such an integral part in the story of *{Bride}* & *{Groom}*, especially friends, that this chapter would be incomplete without your presence, whether you are friends that they know or friends they are yet to know, this is a celebration for you as it is for them. And so I ask those that are present today to affirm your love and support to this couple as they begin this chapter of their story – the story of Husband & Wife.

> Marriage is a commitment to life- to the best that two people can find and bring out in each other. It offers opportunities for sharing and growth no other human relationship can equal, a physical Spiritual and emotional joining that is promised for a lifetime. It offers the opportunity to show up loving, as a reminder to others that they too should aspire for that happiness. It is also a responsibility that a couple takes on to be a living example to their family and friends, to be loving every day in every way and by doing, so raise the energies around them and that of the universe.

> Within the circle of its love, marriage encompasses all of life's most important relationships. A wife and a husband are each other's best friend, confidant, lover, teacher, listener, and critic. There may come times when one partner is heartbroken or ailing, and the love of the other may resemble the tender caring of a parent or child.

> Marriage deepens and enriches every facet of life. Happiness is fuller, memories are fresher, commitment is stronger, even anger is felt more strongly, and passes away more quickly. It is a continuing saga of lessons and a recognition to let go of the event and see the greater lesson.

Marriage understands and forgives the mistakes life is unable to avoid. It encourages and nurtures new life, new experiences, and new ways of expressing love through the seasons of life.

When two people pledge to love and care for each other in marriage, they create a spirit unique to themselves and to all who show up around them, which binds them closer than any spoken or written words. Marriage is a promise, a potential, made in the hearts of two people who love, which takes a lifetime to fulfill.

OFFICIANT: {*Groom*}, please repeat after me:
I, {*Groom*}, take you, {*Bride*}, to be my wife, my partner in life and my unconditional love.
I will cherish our friendship and love you today, tomorrow, and forever.
I will trust you and honor you. I will always create a safe place for you to speak your mind.
I will love you faithfully through the best and the worst as much as I am capable of loving.
No matter what may come, I will always be there.
As I have given you my hand to hold, so I give you my love to drink to quench your thirst.

OFFICIANT: {*Bride*}, please repeat after me:
I, {*Bride*}, take you, {*Groom*}, to be my husband, my partner in life and my one true love.
I will cherish our friendship and love you today, tomorrow, and forever.
I will trust you and honor you. I will always create a safe place for you to speak your mind.
I will love you faithfully through the best and the worst as much as I am capable of loving.
No matter what may come, I will always be there.
As I have given you my hand to hold, so I give you my love to drink

to quench your thirst.

OFFICIANT: {*Groom*}, the woman who stands in front of you is about to become your wife. She will look to you for gentleness, for support, for understanding, for encouragement, continued growth and for protection. You must never take {*Bride*} for granted, but be continually sensitive to her needs. Your life and love will be {*Bride*}'s greatest source of joy.

So I ask you, {*Groom*}, will you have {*Bride*} to be your lawfully wedded wife? Will you love and cherish her? Will you always uphold her and encourage her? Will you be loyal to her and true? Will you honor her all her days and be respectful of her, and promise to always bestow upon her your heart's deepest devotion?

Groom: I will.

OFFICIANT: {*Bride*}, the man who stands in front of you is about to become your husband. He will look to you for gentleness, for support, for understanding, for encouragement, continued growth and for protection. You must never take {*Groom*} for granted, but be continually sensitive to his needs. Your life and love will be {*Groom*}'s greatest source of joy.

So I ask you, {*Bride*}, will you have, {*Groom*}, to be your lawfully wedded husband? Will you love and cherish him? Will you always uphold him and encourage him? Will you be loyal to him and true? Will you honor him all his days and be respectful of him, and promise to always bestow upon him your heart's deepest devotion?

Bride: I will.

OFFICIANT: {*Groom*} & {*Bride*}, please hold each other's hands. These are the hands of your best friend. These are the hands that will love you and cherish you through the years, for a lifetime of happiness. These are the hands that will hold you tight as you struggle through difficult times. These are the hands that will comfort you when you are sick, or console you when you are grieving. These are the hands that will hold you in joy and excitement and hope. These are the hands that will give you support and encouragement to chase down your dreams. Together as a team, everything you wish for can be realized.

OFFICIANT: May I have the rings please? These rings are a token of your love and devotion for each other. May these rings be blessed as a symbol of your affectionate unity. Your two lives are being joined today in one unbroken circle. Wherever you go, may you always return to one another in your togetherness. May you find in one another the love that fulfills all of your wants and needs. May you grow in understanding and compassion. May these rings, soon to be on your fingers, symbolize the loving spirit that is in both your hearts.

OFFICIANT: {*Groom*}, please place the ring on {*Bride*}'s finger and repeat after me:
I give you this ring as a symbol of my love, and with all that I am, and all that I have, I pledge to you my everlasting love. May it be a reminder to you that I hold your heart in my care all the days of my life.

OFFICIANT: {*Bride*}, please place the ring on {*Groom*}'s finger and repeat after me:
I give you this ring as a symbol of my love, and with all that I am, and all that I have, I pledge to you my everlasting love. May it be a reminder to you that I hold your heart in my care all the days of my life.

PRAYER: to be read by family member

OFFICIANT: It is our prayer and hope today that those of you who have taken the vows of marriage will witness the love of {*Groom*} & {*Bride*}, and that hearing their vows will remind you of the love that you have in your relationship... So, on this beautiful February evening, I would like to offer this opportunity for couples to renew their commitment to one another or if you are not here with your partner, or you are single at this time, that you renew the love you have for yourself Please turn inward or towards your partner, take each others' hands, and look into each others' eyes (or close your eyes if single). Erase any of the hurts and pains that you may have experienced in the past, completely releasing them. Recommit to each other or yourself today by repeating after me:

I lovingly recommit my life to you and I vow to be a loving, true, and selfless partner... for all the rest of our days.

OFFICIANT: Perhaps this recommitment will strengthen the bonds of love that have been growing between the two of you or within yourself. If this should happen, I am sure it would be one of the greatest gifts {*Groom*} & {*Bride*} could offer you on their wedding day.

{*Bride*} & {*Groom*}, you have consented together to marriage before this beautiful group of friends, pledged your love and declared your unity by each giving and receiving a ring, and, as you are now joined together in your mutual esteem and devotion, it is my privilege as an Ordained minister of the state of Arizona to pronounce you Husband and Wife.

You may kiss your Bride!

OFFICIANT: Ladies and gentleman, I present to you Mr. & Mrs. _____!!

Ceremony 5 – Unity Earth and Roses to Mothers

Music plays (provided by the chapel) - All rise
Groom up front; Mother of Bride walks in; Bride walks in with Father.

OFFICIANT: You may be seated. Who gives {*Bride*} to be married to {*Groom*}?

Father of Bride: Her mother and I do.

OFFICIANT: At the beginning of this relationship, there was one theme that both believed in: "Love Me, Love My Dogs". It was the common bond between them that brought them together. It is with the love they share with each other and the dogs they have lost and that fills their home with joy, that they walk this path together.

It is one of life's greatest things when two souls meet and lead them to proceed together along a path of marriage. It is indeed one of life's finest experiences. All of us gathering here give witness to the love and commitment they are about to express. As they take their next step into the journey of husband and wife, it is important for all of us here today to support them and for them to feel the love we hold for them today. Let us all unite and make this the day of their dreams.

OFFICIANT: So I ask you, {*Bride*}, will you have {*Groom*} to be your lawfully wedded husband? Will you love and cherish him? Will you always uphold and encourage him? Will you keep him in sickness and health? Will you be loyal to him and true?

Bride: Sure.

OFFICIANT: {*Groom*}, the woman who stands by your side is about to become your wife. She will look to you for gentleness, support, understanding, encouragement, protection and many back rubs. Your life and love will be {*Bride*}'s greatest source of joy.

So I ask, {*Groom*}, will you have {*Bride*} to be your lawfully wedded wife? Will you love and cherish her? Will you always uphold and encourage her? Will you keep her in sickness and health? Will you be loyal to her and true?

Groom: Ditto.

OFFICIANT: {*Groom*}, please repeat after me:
{*Bride*}, I give you this ring as a symbol of my love, and with all that I am and all that I have, I pledge to you my faithful love. May it be a reminder to you that I hold your heart in my care all the days of my life. Today before God and all these witnesses, I, {*Groom*}, take you, {*Bride*}, to be my wife, to laugh with you in joy, to grieve with you in sorrow, to grow old with you in love, to bring you peace, and nurture your spirit.

OFFICIANT: {*Bride*}, please repeat after me:
{*Groom*}, I give you this ring as a symbol of my love, and with all that I am and all that I have, I pledge to you my faithful love. May it be a reminder to you that I hold your heart in my care all the days of my life. Today before God and all these witnesses, I, {*Bride*}, take you, {*Groom*}, to be my husband, to laugh with you in joy, to grieve with you in sorrow, to grow old with you in love, to bring you peace, and nurture your spirit.

PRAYER
OFFICIANT: God bless these hands. May they always be held by one another. Give them strength to hold on during the bad times. May they always reach out to each other for comfort and support. May {*Groom*} and {*Bride*} see their four hands as healer, protector, shelter and guide. Amen.

UNITY EARTH

OFFICIANT: {*Groom*} and {*Bride*}, you have learned much in your individual lives. Your families brought you life and taught you your first lessons about love. Everyone here with you today has been a part of your individual lives, and has shared your hopes, dreams, triumphs and sufferings. Then you met one another. There is a special way that you are together that is not like the way you have ever been with anyone else. You have a way of sharing with each other, of laughing, and joking together that is unlike with anyone else. As your lives come together in unity, your families will also unite to share in your joy. As a symbol of the blending of two lives, two families and a gathering of friends, you have asked that everyone here bring you dirt from across the miles to combine together to symbolize the blending of Earth and soil that nurtures life.

[Earth will now be combined in the glass container].

{Groom} and *{Bride}*:With this soil, we will plant a plant and watch it grow as we grow old together in love. We thank everyone for being a part of our special union.

GIVING A ROSE TO THE MOTHERS

OFFICIANT: Marriage is a coming together of two lives, and a celebration of the love of two people. But it is more. The love that you feel for one another is the flowering of a seed your Mother and Father planted in your hearts many years ago. When you were first born, you were a bundle of diapers and tears, and your parents lost sleep caring for you. Their love for you has brought them great happiness and great challenges, and their love did not diminish as they met these challenges. That is the great lesson that you can bring into your marriage. {*Groom*} and {*Bride*}, as you embrace one another in love, so too do you embrace the families that have been brought together on this happy occasion. As a token of your gratitude for your families, I would like for you now to offer these flowers, as symbols of eternal love, to your Mothers.

OFFICIANT: Robert Browning wrote: "Come my love, grow old along with me, the best is yet to be."
Now that {*Groom*} and {*Bride*} have given themselves to each other by solemn vows, with the joining of hands and the giving and receiving of a ring, it is my privilege as an ordained minister to pronounce that you are husband and wife... FOR-E-VER!

You may now kiss the Bride.

It gives me great pleasure to introduce to you for the first time as husband and wife, Mr. & Mrs. _____!!

<u>Ceremony 6 – Celtic Knot/Flame of Love theme</u>

Processional
-Friend escorts Mother of the Groom to her seat with Father of the Groom following behind them
-Friend escorts Mother of the Bride to her seat
-Officiant takes her place
-Groom and Best Man proceed up right side of the chapel to the front
-Ring Bearer proceeds in and takes his place by Groom and Best Man
-Flower Girl proceeds in scattering petals along the aisle on her way

(Music changes, everybody stands; Bride and Father of the Bride enter)

(After processional – Bride, Groom and Parents of Bride and Groom all remain standing)

OFFICIANT: Please be seated

OFFICIANT: {*Bride*} & {*Groom*}, you have come to this place to join freely in a commitment of love. Who has helped you to come to this place?

Parents of Bride and Groom: "We have."

(Parents of Groom sit)

(Parents of Bride kiss Bride and father gives Bride's hand over to Groom)

(Parents of Bride take seats)

OFFICIANT: {*Bride*}, the flowers you carry remind us of the Brides of Creation in all the seasons and of the springtime of your life together that begins today. Please share with {*Groom*} a token of your commitment.

(Bride takes Groom's boutonniere out of her bouquet, handing her bouquet to Officiant and then pinning the boutonniere on Groom)

(Bride & Groom face each other, join hands)

OFFICIANT: Life is a story that endlessly unfolds - today we have gathered together as {*Bride*} & {*Groom*} choose to join their stories and continue to create an entirely new story.

Like so many, their story begins with an accidental meeting; two lovers finding each other for the first time; two ancient souls, united again to renew the flames of love. Those of you here today have played such an integral part in the story of {Bride} & {Groom} that this chapter would be wholly incomplete without your presence and participation.

But, the story of {*Bride*} & {*Groom*} is not one of fated lovers rediscovering each other on a hot summer Arizona night; it is not of the struggles of a couple to define themselves within a committed relationship and it is not the story of this Blessed Day. For while all those events have shaped this couple, the story of {Bride} & {Groom} is one that is yet to be written.

It is not the tale of loves past, but of the great love that is present now and forever more. It is not the rumination of past triumphs, but rather the constant unfolding of an ever-present love that is now and forever more.

And so I ask those that are present today- those that have meant so much to {*Bride*} *&* {*Groom*}- to affirm your love and commitment to this couple as they begin this chapter of their story – the story of Wife & Husband.

OFFICIANT: We are here to witness the creation of a marriage. Please join me by saying:

"We promise to support {*Bride*} *&* {*Groom*} in their life together."

OFFICIANT: Before they exchange vows, {*Bride*} *&* {*Groom*} would like to share with you the meaning of their love for each other.

(Officiant hands Groom his sheet "prelude to vows" and Groom reads them.)

Groom: I have searched for you all my life. All the many places I have been, all the
things that I have done, have prepared me for this moment. I have tried and
failed. I have searched and never found. And then I found you.

I wasn't looking. The last thing I was looking for was my future. And yet, there you were. In the last place I ever thought to look...right in front of me.

I come here today with all my scars. I've struggled with accepting the happiness I have found in loving you. I've made it so difficult for you, and still you loved me. Loved me with an unconditional love that has overwhelmed all my fears. And so, today, I pledge to you my love, my constant devotion, and my ever-present support.

{*Bride*}, you have taught me a new, a real understanding of love. Today, I pledge to you, that I will love you, I will support you in all you do, and I will cherish you. Together, we will realize the future we wrote, when our souls first merged, at the beginning of time. Now, let us join together, heart and soul, forever.

I love you.

(Officiant hands Bride her sheet "prelude to vows" and Bride reads them.)

Bride: My love, since the first time we met, you have overwhelmed me with your

words. Yet as much as I love your words, it is the small acts of love that have

endeared you to me. I love your goodness, your unfailing support, your ability to

see the beauty in all that I do and all that I am.

I have loved you since before there was time and I will love you until this world dissolves into the Divine.

Today I pledge to you my love, my trust and my future.

I love you.

OFFICIANT: {*Groom*}, repeat after me:

{*Bride*}, I Love You with my whole heart
You are my Soul Mate and so much more
I promise to Love You
To Cherish you
To Nurture you
And to Support you
In all that you are and all that you do
My vow to you today
Is both simple and overwhelming
I will Love You with my whole heart and my whole soul forever
Today it is my great joy
To join you as your husband

OFFICIANT: {*Bride*}, repeat after me:
{*Groom*}, I Love You with my whole heart
You are my Soul Mate and so much more
I promise to Love You
To Cherish you
To Nurture you
And to Support you
In all that you are and all that you do
My vow to you today
Is both simple and overwhelming
I will Love You with my whole heart and my whole soul forever
Today it is my great joy
To join you as your wife

(At the end of the vows, Best Man takes the rings off of the pillow and holds them until further direction.)

OFFICIANT: {*Bride*} *&* {*Groom*} have chosen as a symbol of this day an ancient
Celtic knot: the Trinity knot. Throughout history this icon has meant many things

to many people. To some it symbolized the three phases of life; to others the

three faces of the Divine. {Bride} and {Groom}, you have chosen this symbol

because it reminds you of your commitment to each other in body, mind and

spirit. Let this powerful symbol, beautifully cast into the rings you are about to

exchange, be a constant reminder of this day and what your love means to each

other.

(OFFICIANT gets the rings from Groom)

OFFICIANT: The love that *{Bride}* & *{Groom}* share is a gift of the Divine. It has

filled their hearts with love and their souls with a passion for each other. Now let

that same Spirit fill these rings and provide {Bride} & {Groom} with a constant

wellspring of Divine love throughout the years of their life together.

OFFICIANT: *{Groom}*, repeat after me:
{Bride}, wear this ring as a token
of my undying love for you
and as a symbol of the commitment
I have made to you today.

(Groom places the ring on Bride's finger)

OFFICIANT: *{Bride}*, repeat after me:
{Groom}, wear this ring as a token
of my undying love for you
and as a symbol of the commitment

I have made to you today.

(Bride places the ring on Groom's finger)

OFFICIANT: The flame of Love
The flame of Life
Has been passed from the parents of {*Bride*} and {*Groom*} onto
{*Bride*} & {*Groom*}

(When Officiant says "flame", it is the key for fathers of the Bride
and Groom to light the candles that mothers of the Bride and
Groom are holding.)

OFFICIANT: It is our wish that the model of each of these couple's
steadfast love
will be a light in the darkness for {*Bride*} & {*Groom*}

(Mothers of Bride and Groom pass the candles to Bride & Groom)

*(Bride & Groom go to the Unity candle and light it. After extinguishing their
separate candles they return to their places.)*

OFFICIANT: It is my privilege as a representative of this
community to confirm
your commitment to each other as loving spouses.

OFFICIANT: {*Bride*} & {*Groom*}, please seal your union with a
kiss.

OFFICIANT: It is now my pleasure to introduce, for the first time
as a married
couple, my friends, {*Bride*} & {*Groom*}.

Ceremony 7 – Non-Traditional Ceremony – Child, Hand Blessing and Recommitment theme

OFFICIANT: Thank you for being here today to share in this special ceremony for {*Bride*} and {*Groom*}.

All of us gathering here this beautiful October evening give witness to the love and commitment they are about to express as they take their next step into the journey of husband and wife.

Life is a story that endlessly unfolds – today we have gathered as {*Bride*} & {*Groom*} choose to join their stories and create a new chapter. It is one of life's greatest blessings when two souls meet and lead them along a path of marriage. It is indeed one of life's finest experiences. Their story begins unlike many others. Two souls looking for a home. A place to feel comforted, supported and accepted.

Yet, life is filled with uncertainty. The search for security almost seems an illusion. Stepping in to the uncertainty of life is fertile ground of pure creativity and freedom. Uncertainty means stepping into the unknown in every moment of our existence. The unknown is the field of all possibilities, ever fresh, ever new, always open to the creation of new manifestations. This means that in every moment in your life, you will have excitement, adventure and mystery. You will experience the fun of life – the magic, the celebration, the exhilaration, the exultation of your own spirit. Before you today are two loving souls who are willing to step into a world of uncertainty… together.

Each and every one of you has played such an integral part in the story of {*Bride*} & {*Groom*} that this chapter would be incomplete without your presence. And so I ask those that are present today- those that have meant so much to {*Groom*} & {*Bride*}- to affirm your love and support to this couple as they begin this chapter of their story – the story of Husband & Wife.

Marriage is a commitment to life- to the best that two people can find and bring out in each other. It offers opportunities for sharing and growth no other human relationship can equal, a physical and emotional joining that is promised for a lifetime.

Within the circle of its love, marriage encompasses all of life's most important relationships. A wife and a husband are each other's best friend, confidant, lover, teacher, listener, and critic. There may come times when one partner is heartbroken or ailing, and the love of the other may resemble the tender caring of a parent or child.

Marriage deepens and enriches every facet of life. Happiness is fuller, memories are fresher, commitment is stronger, even anger is felt more strongly, and passes away more quickly.

Marriage understands and forgives the mistakes life is unable to avoid. It encourages and nurtures new life, new experiences, and new ways of expressing love through the seasons of life.

When two people pledge to love and care for each other in marriage, they create a spirit unique to themselves, which binds them closer than any spoken or written words. Marriage is a promise, a potential, made in the hearts of two people who love, which takes a lifetime to fulfill.

OFFICIANT: {*Groom*}, please repeat after me:
I, {*Groom*}, take you, {*Bride*}, to be my wife, my partner in life and my one true love.
I will cherish our friendship and love you today, tomorrow, and forever.

I will trust you and honor you.

I will love you faithfully through the best and the worst.

No matter what may come, I will always be there.

As I have given you my hand to hold, so I give you my life to keep.

OFFICIANT: {*Bride*}, please repeat after me:

I, {*Bride*}, take you, {*Groom*}, to be my husband, my partner in life and my one true love.

I will cherish our friendship and love you today, tomorrow, and forever.

I will trust you and honor you.

I will love you faithfully through the best and the worst.

No matter what may come, I will always be there.

As I have given you my hand to hold, so I give you my life to keep.

VOWS

OFFICIANT: {*Groom*}, the woman who stands in front of you is about to become your wife. She will look to you for gentleness, for support, for understanding, for encouragement, and for protection. You must never take {*Bride*} for granted, but be continually sensitive to her needs. Your life and love will be {*Bride*}'s greatest source of joy.

So I ask you, {*Groom*}, will you have {*Bride*} to be your lawfully wedded wife? Will you love and cherish her? Will you always uphold her and encourage her? Will you be loyal to her and true? Will you honor her all her days and be respectful of her, and promise to always bestow upon her your heart's deepest devotion?

Groom: I will.

OFFICIANT: {*Bride*}, the man who stands in front of you is about to become your husband. He will look to you for gentleness, for support, for understanding, for encouragement, and for protection.

You must never take {*Groom*} for granted, but be continually sensitive to his needs. Your life and love will be {*Groom*}'s greatest source of joy.

So I ask you, {*Bride*}, will you have {*Groom*} to be your lawfully wedded husband? Will you love and cherish him? Will you always uphold him and encourage him? Will you be loyal to him and true? Will you honor him all his days and be respectful of him, and promise to always bestow upon him your heart's deepest devotion?

Bride: I will.

HAND BLESSING

OFFICIANT: {*Groom*} & {*Bride*}, please hold each other's hands. These are the hands of your best friend. These are the hands that will love you and cherish you through the years, for a lifetime of happiness. These are the hands that will hold you tight as you struggle through difficult times. These are the hands that will comfort you when you are sick, or console you when you are grieving. These are the hands that will hold you in joy and excitement and hope. These are the hands that will give you support and encouragement to chase down your dreams. Together as a team, everything you wish for can be realized.

RINGS

OFFICIANT: May I have the rings please? These rings are a token of your love and devotion for each other. May these rings be blessed as a symbol of your affectionate unity. Your two lives are being joined today in one unbroken circle. Wherever you go, may you always return to one another in your togetherness. May you find in one another the love that fulfills all of your wants and needs. May you grow in understanding and compassion. May these rings, soon to be on your fingers, symbolize the loving spirit that is in both your hearts.

OFFICIANT: {*Groom*}, please place the ring on {*Bride*}'s finger and repeat after me:

I give you this ring as a symbol of my love, and with all that I am, and all that I have, I pledge to you my everlasting love. May it be a reminder to you that I hold your heart in my care all the days of my life.

OFFICIANT: {*Bride*}, please place the ring on {*Groom*}'s finger and repeat after me:

I give you this ring as a symbol of my love, and with all that I am, and all that I have, I pledge to you my everlasting love. May it be a reminder to you that I hold your heart in my care all the days of my life.

OFFICIANT: Today, as {*Bride*} and {*Groom*} are becoming man and wife, they are also becoming a family. To symbolize this, {*Groom*} has a gift and a vow for {*Bride's Daughter*} as well.

OFFICIANT: {*Groom*}, please repeat after me:

Today, as I marry your mother, we enter into a life together as a family. I am honored and blessed today to share with you my love! I promise to you, {*Bride's Daughter*}, that I will always be there to nurture, love and support you. I will always recognize the light you are in our lives!

PRAYER

OFFICIANT: It is our prayer and hope today that those of you who have taken the vows of marriage will witness the love of {*Groom*} & {*Bride*}, and that hearing their vows will remind you of the love that you have in your relationship…

So, on the beautiful October evening, I would like to offer this opportunity for couples to renew their commitment to one another, or if you are not here with your partner or you are single at this time, that you renew the love you have for yourself. Please turn inward or towards your partner, take each others' hands, and look into each others' eyes (or close your eyes if single). Erase any of the hurts and pains that you may have experienced in the past, completely releasing them.

Recommit to each other or yourself today by repeating after me:

I lovingly recommit my life to you and I vow to be a loving, true, and selfless partner… for all the rest of our days.

OFFICIANT: Perhaps this recommitment will strengthen the bonds of love that have been growing between the two of you or within yourself. If this should happen, I am sure it would be one of the greatest gifts {*Groom*} & {*Bride*} could offer you on their wedding day.

OFFICIANT: Today, {*Bride*} & {*Groom*} have chosen to commemorate their marriage through the celebration of the Sand Ceremony. This ceremony symbolizes the inseparable union of {*Bride*} & {*Groom*} into a new and eternal marital relationship as well as into a family. {*Bride*}, {*Groom*} and {*Bride's Daughter*} will each pour separate containers of sand into a common vessel. Each grain of sand in their separate containers represents a unique and separate moment, decision, feeling or event that helped shaped {*Bride*} and {*Groom*} into the separate and unique individuals that they are today. As they pour their separate containers of sand into a common vessel, those separate and independent individuals will cease to exist. Instead they will merge into a loving and supportive family of three. {*Bride*} & {*Groom*}, just as the grains of sand can never be separated into their individual containers again, so will your lives be changed forever from this day forward, into the beautiful family you have chosen and created.

{*Bride*} & {*Groom*}, you have consented together to marriage before this beautiful group of friends and family, pledged your love and declared your unity by each giving and receiving a ring, and, as you are now joined together in your mutual esteem and devotion, it is my privilege as an Ordained minister of the state of Arizona to pronounce you Husband and Wife.

You may kiss your Bride!

OFFICIANT: Ladies and gentleman, I present to you Mr. & Mrs. _____!!

Ceremony 8 – Children and Unity Sand

OPENING WORDS OF THE OFFICIANT
OFFICIANT: Friends, we have been invited here today to share with {*Bride*} and {*Groom*} a very important moment in their lives. In the years they have been together, their love and understanding of each other has grown and matured, and now they have decided to live their lives together as husband and wife.

THE GIVING IN MARRIAGE
OFFICIANT: Who supports this woman in her marriage to this man?

Father of the Bride: "Her mother and I."

OPENING READING

OFFICIANT: Thank you for being here today to share in this special ceremony for {*Bride*} and {*Groom*}.

All of us gathering here this beautiful March evening give witness to the love and commitment they are about to express as they take their next step into the journey of husband and wife.

Everyone plays such an integral part in the story of {*Bride*} and {*Groom*}, especially their daughters, but this chapter would be incomplete without the presence of their extended families and closest friends. This is a celebration for you as it is for them. And so I ask those that are present today, to affirm your love and support to this couple as they begin this chapter of their story – the story of Husband & Wife.

Marriage is a commitment to life- to the best that two people can find and bring out in each other. It offers opportunities for sharing and growth no other human relationship can equal; a physical, spiritual and emotional joining that is promised for a lifetime. It offers the opportunity to show up loving, as a reminder to others that they too should aspire for that happiness. It is also a responsibility that a couple takes on to be a living example to their family and friends, to be loving every day in every way and by doing so, raise the energies around them and that of the universe.

Within the circle of its love, marriage encompasses all of life's most important relationships. A wife and a husband are each other's best friend, confidant, lover, teacher, listener, and critic. There may come times when one partner is heartbroken or ailing, and the love of the other may resemble the tender caring of a parent or child.

Marriage deepens and enriches every facet of life. Happiness is fuller, memories are fresher, commitment is stronger, even anger is felt more strongly, and passes away more quickly. It is a continuing saga of lessons and a recognition to let go of the event and see the greater lesson.

Marriage understands and forgives the mistakes life is unable to avoid. It encourages and nurtures new life, new experiences, and new ways of expressing love through the seasons of life.

When two people pledge to love and care for each other in marriage, they create a spirit unique to themselves and to all who show up around them, which binds them closer than any spoken or written words. Marriage is a promise, a potential, made in the hearts of two people who love, which takes a lifetime to fulfill.

INTENTION

OFFICIANT: {*Groom*}, do you take this woman to be your wife? Will you love her, comfort her, honor her, and keep her in sickness and in health; and forsaking all others, be faithful to her as long as you both shall live?

Groom: I do.

OFFICIANT: {*Bride*}, do you take this man to be your husband? Will you love him, comfort him, honor him, and keep him in sickness and in health; and forsaking all others, be faithful to him as long as you both shall live?

Bride: I do.

VOWS

OFFICIANT: {*Groom*}, repeat after me:
{*Bride*}, I Love You with my whole heart
You are my Soul Mate and so much more

I promise to Love You
To Cherish you
To Nurture you
And to Support you
In all that you are and all that you do
My vow to you today
Is both simple and overwhelming
I will Love You with my whole heart and my whole soul forever
Today it is my great joy
To join you as your husband

OFFICIANT: {*Bride*}, repeat after me:
{*Groom*}, I Love You with my whole heart
You are my Soul Mate and so much more
I promise to Love You
To Cherish you
To Nurture you
And to Support you
In all that you are and all that you do
My vow to you today
Is both simple and overwhelming
I will Love You with my whole heart and my whole soul forever
Today it is my great joy
To join you as your wife

VOWS FOR CHILDREN
OFFICIANT: Not only do {*Bride*} and {*Groom*} promise to be a good husband and wife to each other, but they also give promise to be patient and loving parents to {*Children*}.

{*Bride*} and {*Groom*} please repeat after me:
We promise to be loving and kind to our children, to be their strength and their emotional support, loving them with all our hearts forever and always.

EXCHANGE OF RINGS

OFFICIANT: May I have the rings please? These rings are a token of your love and devotion for each other. May these rings be blessed as a symbol of your affectionate unity. Your two lives are being joined today in one unbroken circle. Wherever you go, may you always return to one another in your togetherness. May you find in one another the love that fulfills all of your wants and needs. May you grow in understanding and compassion. May these rings, soon to be on your fingers, symbolize the loving spirit that is in both your hearts.

OFFICIANT: {*Groom*}, please place the ring on {*Bride*}'s finger and repeat after me:
I give you this ring as a symbol of my love, and with all that I am, and all that I have, I pledge to you my everlasting love. May it be a reminder to you that I hold your heart in my care all the days of my life.

OFFICIANT: {*Bride*}, please place the ring on {*Groom*}'s finger and repeat after me:
I give you this ring as a symbol of my love, and with all that I am, and all that I have, I pledge to you my everlasting love. May it be a reminder to you that I hold your heart in my care all the days of my life.

UNITY SAND CEREMONY

OFFICIANT: I'd now like to invite {*Children*} to come up for the Unity Sand ceremony.
Today, this relationship is symbolized through the pouring of this sand, each color representing a member. As each individual's sand is poured into the family's one united container, the individual containers of sand will no longer exist, but will be joined together as one. Just as these grains of sand can never be separated and poured again into the individual containers, so will become the bond with

your family.

OFFICIANT: We begin with a layer of neutral sand which symbolizes that the marriage is grounded.
(*This sand is already in the base of the container.*)

OFFICIANT: Then we layer the individual colors. This symbolizes that the marriage is based on the strength of the individuals.
(*Groom pours some of his sand in, followed by Bride pouring about the same amount, and then each Child pours about the same amount.*)

OFFICIANT: And now we combine the color, which symbolizes all these lives joined as one family together forever.
(*Everyone pours sand into large vase so that the colors combine until their jars are empty.*)

CLOSING

DECLARATION OF MARRIAGE
Now that {*Bride*} and {*Groom*} have given themselves to each other by solemn vows, with the joining of hands and the giving and receiving of a ring, it is my pleasure and by the power vested in me by the State of _____, to now pronounce you husband and wife.

{*Groom*} you may now kiss your Bride!

INTRODUCTION OF NEWLYWEDS
(*This is where music will play*)
Ladies and Gentlemen, I present to you Mr. & Mrs. _____!!
Since the children will already be on stage, they will all exit together as a family.

Ceremony 9 – Non-Traditional Ceremony ('Path of Marriage' theme)

OFFICIANT: You may be seated! Thank you all for being here today to share in this special ceremony for {*Groom*} and {*Bride*}.

OFFICIANT: Who gives {*Bride*} to be married to {*Groom*}?

Father of the Bride: Her mother and I do.

OFFICIANT: It is one of life's greatest things when two souls meet and lead them to proceed together along a path of marriage. It is indeed one of life's finest experiences. All of us gathering here give witness to the love and commitment they are about to express. As they take their next step into the journey of husband and wife, it is important for all of us here today to support them and for them to feel the love we hold for them today. Let us all unite and make this the day of their dreams.

> The little things are the big things.
> It is never being too old to hold hands.
> It is remembering to say "I love you" at least once a day.
> It is never going to sleep angry.
> It is at no time taking the other for granted.
> The courtship should not end with the honeymoon.
> It should continue through all the years.
> It is having a mutual sense of values and common objectives.
> It is standing together facing the world.
> It is forming a circle of love that gathers in the whole family.
> It is doing things for each other, not in the attitude of duty or sacrifice; but in the spirit of joy.
> It is speaking words of appreciation and demonstrating gratitude in thoughtful ways.
> It is not expecting too much from one another.

It is always seeing the good in each other.

It is cultivating flexibility, patience, understanding, and a sense of humor.

It is having the capacity to forgive and forget.

It is giving each other an atmosphere in which each can grow.

It is finding room for the things of the spirit.

It is a common search for the good and the beautiful.

It is establishing a relationship in which the independence is equal; dependence is mutual and the obligation is reciprocal.

It is not only marrying the right partner; it is being the right partner.

Marriage is more than a contract. It is a commitment to take joy deep into the discovery of who you most truly are. It is a commitment to a spiritual journey, to a life of becoming.

Marriage is a covenant that says:

I love you;

I trust you;

I will be here for you when you are hurting;

And when I am hurting I will not leave.

It is not a place where we run from pain, anger or sorrow, but rather a safe sanctuary to risk loving, to risk living, and sharing from the center of oneself.

OFFICIANT: {*Groom*}, the woman standing by your side is about to become your wife. She will look to you for gentleness, for support, for understanding, for encouragement, and for protection. You must never take {*Bride*} for granted, and be continually sensitive to her needs. Your life and love will be {*Bride*}'s greatest source of joy.

So I ask you, {*Groom*}, will you have {*Bride*} to be your lawfully wedded wife? Will you love and cherish her? Will you always uphold her and encourage here? Will you be loyal to her and true? Will you honor her all her days and be respectful of her, and promise to always bestow upon her your heart's deepest devotion?

Groom: I will.

OFFICIANT: {*Bride*}, the man standing by your side is about to become your husband. He will look to you for gentleness, for support, for understanding, for encouragement, and for protection. You must never take {*Groom*} for granted, and be continually sensitive to his needs. Your life and love will be {*Groom*}'s greatest source of joy.

So I ask you, {*Bride*}, will you have {*Groom*} to be your lawfully wedded husband? Will you love and cherish him? Will you always uphold him and encourage him? Will you be loyal to him and true? Will you honor him all his days and be respectful of him, and promise to always bestow upon him your heart's deepest devotion?

Bride: I will.

OFFICIANT: {*Groom*}, please hold {*Bride*}'s hand.
These are the hands of your best friend. These are the hands the will passionately love you and cherish you through the years, for a lifetime of happiness. These are the hands that will hold you tight as you struggle through difficult times. These are the hands that will comfort you when you are sick, or console you when you are grieving. These are the hands that will hold you in joy and excitement and hope. These are the hands that will give you support as she encourages you to chase down your dreams. Together as a team, everything you wish for can be realized.

OFFICIANT: {*Groom*}, please repeat after me:
Today before God and all these witnesses, I, {*Groom*}, take you, {*Bride*}, to be my wife. To laugh with you in joy, to grieve with you in sorrow, to grow with you in love, to bring you peace and nurture your spirit.

OFFICIANT: {*Bride*}, as you face {*Groom*}:

These are the hands of your best friend, strong and vibrant with love. Holding your hand on your wedding day as he promises to love you all the days of his life. These are the hands that will work alongside yours as together you build your future, as you laugh and cry, as you share your innermost secrets and dreams. These are the hands that will love you and cherish you through the years for a lifetime of happiness. These are the hands that will countless times wipe the tears from your eyes – tears of sorrow and tears of joy. These are the hands that will comfort you in illness and hold you when you are frightened or grieving. These are the hands that will tenderly lift your chin and brush your cheek as they raise your face to look into your eyes – eyes that are filled completely with his overwhelming love and desire for you.

OFFICIANT: {*Bride*}, please repeat after me:

Today before God and all these witnesses, I, {*Bride*}, take you, {*Groom*}, to be my husband. To laugh with you in joy, to grieve with you in sorrow, to grow with you in love, to bring you peace and nurture your spirit.

OFFICIANT: God bless these hands. May they always be held by one another. Give them strength to hold on during the bad times. Keep them tender and gentle. May {*Groom*} and {*Bride*} see their four hands as healing, protection, shelter, and guidance. Amen.

OFFICIANT: May I have the rings please? As you offer these rings, it is a token of your love and devotion for each other. May these rings be blessed as a symbol of this affectionate unity. Your two lives are being joined today in one unbroken circle. Wherever you go, may you always return to one another in your togetherness. May you find in one another the love for which all men and women yearn. May you grow in understanding and compassion. May these rings symbolize the touch of the spirit of love that is in both your hearts.

OFFICIANT: {*Groom*}, please repeat after me:

{*Bride*}, I give you this ring as a symbol of my love, and with all that I am and all that I have, I pledge my faithful love. May it be a reminder to you that I hold your heart in my care all the days of my life.

OFFICIANT: {*Bride*}, please repeat after me:

{*Groom*}, I give you this ring as a symbol of my love, and with all that I am and all that I have, I pledge my faithful love. May it be a reminder to you that I hold your heart in my care all the days of my life.

OFFICIANT:Now that {*Groom*} and {*Bride*} have given themselves to each other by solemn vows, with the joining of hands and the giving and receiving of a ring, it is my privilege as an ordained minister to pronounce that you are husband and wife.

You may now kiss the Bride!

It gives me great pleasure to introduce to you for the first time as husband and wife, Mr. & Mrs. _____!!

Ceremony 10 – Handfasting Ceremony

Getting into position: Officiant comes down across bridge and under archway and tells everyone that the wedding is about to commence.

Someone cues the bagpiper.

Groom comes across bridge and takes his spot, through arch to left side (facing crowd).

Best Man comes across bridge and takes his spot, next to Groom.

Maid of Honor comes across bridge and under archway to right side.

Mother will carry Flower Girl across bridge and through arch, then take her spot in front row.

Mother will carry Ring Bearer across bridge and through arch, handing off rings to Best Man, then take her seat in front row.
Son of the Bride will escort Bride over bridge and through arch, kiss his mother and shake Groom's hand. Then take his seat in front row.

OFFICIANT: You may be seated! Thank you all for being here today to share in this special ceremony for {*Groom*} and {*Bride*}.

OFFICIANT: It is one of life's greatest things when two souls meet and lead them to proceed together along a path of marriage. It is indeed one of life's finest experiences. All of us gathering here give witness to the love and commitment they are about to express. As they take their next step into the journey of husband and wife, it is important for all of us here today to support them and for them to feel the love we hold for them today. Let us all unite and make this the day of their dreams.

> The little things are the big things.
> It is never being too old to hold hands.
> It is remembering to say "I love you" at least once a day.
> It is never going to sleep angry.
> It is at no time taking the other for granted.
> The courtship should not end with the honeymoon.
> It should continue through all the years.
> It is having a mutual sense of values and common objectives.
> It is standing together facing the world.
> It is forming a circle of love that gathers in the whole family.
> It is doing things for each other, not in the attitude of duty or sacrifice; but in the spirit of joy.
> It is speaking words of appreciation and demonstrating gratitude in thoughtful ways.
> It is not expecting too much from one another.
> It is always seeing the good in each other.
> It is cultivating flexibility, patience, understanding, and a

sense of humor.

It is having the capacity to forgive and forget.

It is giving each other an atmosphere in which each can grow.

It is finding room for the things of the spirit.

It is a common search for the good and the beautiful.

It is establishing a relationship in which the independence is equal, dependence is mutual and the obligation is reciprocal.

It is not only marrying the right partner; it is being the right partner.

Marriage is more than a contract. It is a commitment to take joy deep into the discovery of who you most truly are. It is a commitment to a spiritual journey, to a life of becoming.

Marriage is a covenant that says:

I love you;

I trust you;

I will be here for you when you are hurting;

And when I am hurting I will not leave.

It is not a place where we run from pain, anger or sorrow, but rather a safe sanctuary to risk loving, to risk living, and sharing from the center of oneself.

OFFICIANT: {*Groom*}, the woman standing by your side is about to become your wife. She will look to you for gentleness, for support, for understanding, for encouragement, and for protection. You must never take {*Bride*} for granted, and be continually sensitive to her needs.

So I ask you, {*Groom*}, will you have {*Bride*} to be your lawfully wedded wife? Will you love and cherish her? Will you always uphold her and encourage here? Will you be loyal to her and true? Will you honor her all her days and be respectful of her, and promise to always bestow upon her your heart's deepest devotion?

Groom: I will.

OFFICIANT: {*Bride*}, the man standing by your side is about to become your husband. He will look to you for gentleness, for support, for understanding, for encouragement, and for protection. You must never take {*Groom*} for granted, and be continually sensitive to his needs.

So I ask you, {*Bride*}, will you have {*Groom*} to be your lawfully wedded husband? Will you love and cherish him? Will you always uphold him and encourage him? Will you be loyal to him and true? Will you honor him all his days and be respectful of him, and promise to always bestow upon him your heart's deepest devotion?

Bride: I will.

OFFICIANT: {*Bride*} and {*Groom*} have chosen a traditional hand fasting ceremony. In Europe, until the mid 1700's, few unions were sanctified in a church or synagogue. Rather, they were celebrated by a simple hand fasting ceremony in which the two partners joined hands over the village anvil, in the fields or in the groves of trees. Today, we build upon this tradition. The couple links hands, to form an infinity circle, symbolizing the entirety of the universe as represented in their relationship.

{*Bride*} and {*Groom*}, please join hands in the infinity circle. These are the hands of your best friend. These are the hands the will passionately love you and cherish you through the years, for a lifetime of happiness. These are the hands that will hold you tight as you struggle through difficult times. These are the hands that will comfort you when you are sick, or console you when you are grieving. These are the hands that will hold you in joy and excitement and hope. These are the hands that will give you support as you encourage each other to chase down your dreams. Together, as a team, everything you wish for can be realized.

To Both

OFFICIANT: Will you share each other's pain and seek to ease it?

Bride and Groom: Yes.

OFFICIANT: And so the binding is made. Join your hands.
First cord is draped across the Bride and Groom's hands

To Both
OFFICIANT: Will both of you look for the brightness in life and the positive in each other?

Bride and Groom: Yes.

OFFICIANT: And so the binding is made.
Second chord is draped across the couple's hands

To Both
OFFICIANT: Will you share the burdens of each so that your spirits may grow in this union?

Bride and Groom: Yes.

OFFICIANT: And so the binding is made.
Drape third chord across the couple's hands

To Both
OFFICIANT: Will you dream together to create new realities and hopes?

Bride and Groom: Yes.

OFFICIANT: And so the binding is made.
Drape fourth chord across the couple's hands

To Both
OFFICIANT: Will you take the heat of anger and use it to temper the strength of this union?

Bride and Groom: We will.

OFFICIANT: And so the binding is made.
Drape fifth chord across the couple's hands

To Both
OFFICIANT: Will you seek to never give cause to break that honor?

Bride and Groom: We shall never do so.

OFFICIANT: And so the binding is made.
Drape sixth chord across the couple's hands

Tie chords together while saying:
OFFICIANT: The knots of this binding are not formed by these chords, but instead by your vows. Either of you may drop the chords, for as always, you hold in your own hands the making or breaking of this union.

Once chords are tied together they are removed and given to brother.

OFFICIANT: {*Bride*}, please repeat after me:
Today before God and all these witnesses, I, {*Bride*}, take you, {*Groom*}, to be my husband. To laugh with you in joy, to grieve with you in sorrow, to grow with you in love, to bring you peace and nurture your spirit.
OFFICIANT: {*Groom*}, please repeat after me:
Today before God and all these witnesses, I, {*Groom*}, take you, {*Bride*}, to be my wife. To laugh with you in joy, to grieve with you in

sorrow, to grow with you in love, to bring you peace and nurture your spirit.

OFFICIANT: God bless these hands. May they always be held by one another. Give them strength to hold on during the bad times. Keep them tender and gentle. May {*Groom*} and {*Bride*} see their four hands as healing, protection, shelter, and guidance. Amen.

OFFICIANT: May I have the rings please? As you offer these rings, it is a token of your love and devotion for each other. May these rings be blessed as a symbol of this affectionate unity. Your two lives are being joined today in one unbroken circle. Wherever you go, may you always return to one another in your togetherness. May you find in one another the love for which all men and women yearn. May you grow in understanding and compassion. May these rings symbolize the touch of the spirit of love that is in both your hearts.

OFFICIANT: {*Groom*}, please repeat after me:
{*Bride*}, I give you this ring as a symbol of my love, and with all that I am and all that I have, I pledge my faithful love. May it be a reminder to you that I hold your heart in my care all the days of my life.

OFFICIANT: {*Bride*}, please repeat after me:
{*Groom*}, I give you this ring as a symbol of my love, and with all that I am and all that I have, I pledge my faithful love. May it be a reminder to you that I hold your heart in my care all the days of my life.

OFFICIANT: Now that {*Groom*} and {*Bride*} have given themselves to each other by solemn vows, with the joining of hands and the giving and receiving of a ring, it is my privilege as an ordained minister to pronounce that you are husband and wife.

You may now kiss the Bride!

It gives me great pleasure to introduce to you for the first time as husband and wife, Mr. & Mrs. _____!!

Ceremony 11 – Pagan Wedding Ceremony by Sarah Bliss

OPENING

OFFICIANT: The greatest thing you'll ever learn is just to love and be loved in return. Welcome family and friends. We have been brought here today to share with {*Bride*} and {*Groom*} in this sacred space as they commit to each other in the union of marriage. Each of you represent something special to this couple and it is an honor to help them celebrate as they embark on a journey of love. On behalf of {*Bride*} and {*Groom*}, I want to thank you for being here.

The dictionary definition of the word "love" means a profound tender, passionate affection for one another. Some of the key ingredients in the meaning of life can be found in words of this definition. The greatest thing we'll ever know is to love and be loved in return. And to come together with a commitment of the heart through the sacred act of marriage, is the holiest of ways we honor the definition of love.

{*Bride*} and {*Groom*}, may you fully commitment with not only your hearts and your words today, but by your actions as you move through your lives together. To love without condition or expectation, is the only responsibility we have to one another in this life – just to love and be loved in return.
At this time, I would like to ask you to stand and join me in a prayer.

PRAYER (*everyone stand - alternate, form circle with bridle party*)

OFFICIANT: We gather here this Night (day) to bind a man and woman in a ritual of love. Let all who stand, be here of their own free will and that you come with peace in your heart. We ask that this sacred space be filled with love and consecrated before God and Goddess and may it be a Guardian and Protection for the work we do on this Night (day). Let {*Bride*} and {*Groom*} stand here before us and also in the Presence of the Ancient Ones.

> To the East: Be here with us Spirits of the Air. With your breath of life, join the bonds between these two and tie them tightly.

> To the South: Be here with us Beings of Fire. Give their love and passion all your own consuming devotion.

> To the West: Be here with us Beings of Water. Grant these two the deepest of love; richness of body, soul and spirit.

> To the North: Be here with us Spirits of Earth. Let your strength and constancy be theirs for as long as they desire to be together.

OFFICIANT: Blessed God and Goddess, look with joy upon the Union of this man and this woman. Grant them harmony and beauty in their lives and let them always be mindful of their commitment, one to the other. Let their happiness shine as a beacon for all to see. We thank you for your attendance in our Sacred Ceremony and ask for your blessing upon this couple and upon the commitment they are making here on this Night (day).

Namaste.

VOWS

OFFICIANT: A marriage is an equal partnership, to be set upon whole-heartedly, with full intentions of working together, to ensure that your marriage is long and happy. Marriage offers us an opportunity for sharing and growing no other human relationship can equal. It is a physical and emotional joining that is a promise meant to be kept with compassion, faithfulness and respect.

As you share in your vows, you pledge to one another, that from this day forward, these spoken words will always be in the foreground of your thoughts, will guide your actions, and that you will not leave any parts of yourself unknowable to each other.

OFFICIANT: Let us return our attention to {*Bride*} and {*Groom*} and bear witness as they enter into the holy sacrament of marriage by exchanging their vows.

OFFICIANT: {*Bride*}, repeat after me:
I stand before you today, in the presence of God and Goddess, our family and friends, to offer you my heart in a journey filled with unconditional love. I promise from this day forward, to honor you always, to trust you even in times of struggle, and to respect you for all that you are today and all that you will become tomorrow. I no longer walk this world alone, for today, I am honored to become your wife.

OFFICIANT: Do you take {*Groom*} to be your lawful husband, your faithful partner, to give and to receive, to speak and to listen, to inspire and to respond?

Bride: I do.

OFFICIANT: This is a commitment made in love, kept in faith and eternally made new.

OFFICIANT: {*Groom*}, repeat after me:
I stand before you today, in the presence of God and Goddess, our family and friends, to offer you my heart in a journey filled with unconditional love. I promise from this day forward, to honor you

always, to trust you even in times of struggle, and to respect you for all that you are today and all that you will become tomorrow. I no longer walk this world alone, for today, I am honored to become your husband.

OFFICIANT: Do you take {*Bride*} to be your lawful wife, your faithful partner, to give and to receive, to speak and to listen, to inspire and to respond?

Groom: I do.

OFFICIANT: This is a commitment made in love, kept in faith and eternally made new.

EXCHANGE OF RINGS

OFFICIANT: It was once thought that there was a vein which ran directly from the ring finger of the left hand to the heart, hence the reason tradition would have us wear a wedding ring on the left hand. The circle is a symbol of the sun, the earth and the universe. It is a symbol that represents a union that is meant to last forever and that no matter where you go, you will always return to one another and to your togetherness.

As {*Bride*} and {*Groom*} exchange their wedding rings, they will represent a symbol of unity, in which their lives are now joined in one unbroken circle. May I have the rings please? May these rings be blessed today and always. May these rings symbolize the spirit of love you have for one another and may that love grow stronger with each passing day. May your rings always remind you of the vows you have spoken here today.

OFFICIANT: {*Bride*}, repeat after me:

I give you this ring as a symbol of my never-ending love. I marry you with this ring, with all that I have and all that I am.

OFFICIANT: {*Groom*}, repeat after me:
I give you this ring as a symbol of my never-ending love. I marry you with this ring, with all that I have and all that I am.

CONCLUSION OF CEREMONY
OFFICIANT: Above you are the Stars and below you are the stones. As time passes remember this: like a stone, your love should be firm. Be close, but grant each other freedom to grow. Be understanding and compassionate. Be supportive and nurturing. Share in each other's dreams. Have patience with each other. Be free in giving warmth and affection and never take each for granted. Let the stars that shine above you be as bright as they are today, for all the days of your life. May peace and love be with you.

Let us now celebrate what the Universe has brought together and so it is, and so it shall be!

By the power vested in me, I now pronounce you husband and wife!

You may kiss your Bride!

Ladies and gentlemen, family and friends, it gives me great pleasure to introduce to you for the very first time, Mr. & Mrs. _____!!

Ceremony 12 – Honoring of Deceased Loved One

OFFICIANT: Please rise.

OFFICIANT: You may be seated.

OFFICIANT: Who gives {*Bride*} to be married to {*Groom*}?

Father of the Bride: Her Mother and I.

OFFICIANT: Thank you for coming here today to share in this special ceremony for {Bride} & {Groom}. We have come together on this beautiful October afternoon, in the presence of God, to witness and bless the joining together of this man and woman in holy matrimony. {Bride} and {Groom} are blessed to have so many people here that love and support them. We'd like to take a moment to recognize {Groom's Step Dad} and {Groom's Mother} who are absent physically from this ceremony, due to illness, but are ever present in Spirit. We thank you all for being here and making this a very special day.

{Bride} and {Groom} would like to take a moment to honor those that have passed away and are greatly missed as well. They'd like to specifically honor {Groom's Father} and {Bride's Grandfather}. As they light a candle in remembrance of the very special people that are no longer here, they have asked me to share this poem with you.

> "Although death has separated us physically, faith and love have bound us eternally.
> Though we cannot see you, we know you are here.
> Though we cannot touch you, we feel the warmth of your smile, as we begin a new chapter in our lives.
> Today we pause to reflect upon those who have shaped our character, Molded our spirits and touched our hearts.
> May the lighting of this candle be a reminder of the memories we have shared,
> A representation of the everlasting impact you have made upon our lives."

OFFICIANT: It is one of life's greatest things when two souls meet and lead them to proceed together along a path of marriage. It is indeed one of life's finest experiences. All of us gathering here give witness to the love and commitment they are about to express as they take their next step into the journey of husband and wife. It is important for all of us here today to support them and for them to feel the love we hold for them today.

Please bow your head in prayer:

Bless this marriage, O God, as {*Bride*} and {*Groom*} begin their journey down the road of life together.

We don't know what lies ahead for the road turns and bends. But help them to make the best of whatever comes their way.

Help them to hug each other often, talk and laugh a lot.

Help them to continue to enjoy each other as they did when they first met.

Help them to realize that nothing nor no one is perfect and to look for the good in all things and all people including themselves.

Help them to respect each other's likes and dislikes, opinion and beliefs, hopes and dreams and fears.

Help them to learn from each other and to help each other to grow mentally, emotionally, and spiritually.

Help them to realize that there is design and purpose in their lives as in the world, and if they will hold onto each other, they will know that things have a way of working out for the good.

Help them to create for their children a peaceful, stable home of love as a foundation on which they can build their lives.

But most of all, dear God, help them to keep lit the torch of love that they now share in their hearts so that by their loving example they may pass on the light of love to their children and to their children's children forever. Amen

OFFICIANT: Marriage is a promise of love.

Marriage is a commitment to life- to the best that two people can find and bring out in each other. It offers opportunities for sharing and growth no other human relationship can equal, a physical and emotional joining that is promised for a lifetime.

Within the circle of its love, marriage encompasses all of life's most important relationships. A wife and a husband are each other's best friend, confidant, lover, teacher, listener, and critic. There may come times when one partner is heartbroken or ailing, and the love of the other may resemble the tender caring of a parent or child.

Marriage deepens and enriches every facet of life. Happiness is fuller, memories are fresher, commitment is stronger, even anger is felt more strongly, and passes away more quickly.

Marriage understands and forgives the mistakes life is unable to avoid. It encourages and nurtures new life, new experiences, and new ways of expressing love through the seasons of life.

When two people pledge to love and care for each other in marriage, they create a spirit unique to themselves, which binds them closer than any spoken or written words. Marriage is a promise, a potential, made in the hearts of two people who love, which takes a lifetime to fulfill.

OFFICIANT: {*Groom*}, do you take this woman to be your wife? Will you love her, comfort her, honor her, and keep her in sickness and in health; and forsaking all others, be faithful to her as long as you both shall live?

Groom: I will.

OFFICIANT: {*Bride*}, do you take this man to be your husband? Will you love him, comfort him, honor him, and keep him in sickness and in health; and forsaking all others, be faithful to him as long as you both shall live?

Bride: I will.

VOWS

OFFICIANT: {*Groom*}, please hold hands and repeat after me:
I, {*Groom*}, take you, {*Bride*}, to be my wife, my partner, my friend, my confidant, my soul mate.

OFFICIANT: {*Bride*}, please repeat after me:
I, {*Bride*}, take you, {*Groom*}, to be my husband, my partner, my friend, my confidant, and my soul mate.

OFFICIANT: May I have the rings please? As you offer these rings they are a token of your love and devotion for each other. May these rings be blessed as a symbol of this affectionate unity. Your two lives are being joined today in one unbroken circle. Wherever you go, may you always return to one another in your togetherness. May you find in one another the love for which all men and women yearn. May you grow in understanding and compassion. May these rings, soon to be on your fingers, symbolize the spirit of love that is in both your hearts.

OFFICIANT: {*Groom*}, please place the ring on {*Bride*}'s finger and repeat after me:
I give you this ring as a symbol of my love, and with all that I am, and all that I have, I pledge to you my faithful love.

OFFICIANT: {*Bride*}, please place the ring on {*Groom*}'s finger and repeat after me:
I give you this ring as a symbol of my love, and with all that I am, and all that I have, I pledge to you my faithful love.

OFFICIANT: {*Groom*} & {*Bride*}, you have consented together to marriage before this beautiful group of friends and family, pledged your faith and declared your unity by the giving and receiving of a ring, and, as you are now joined together in your mutual esteem and devotion, it is my privilege as an Ordained minister of the state of Arizona to pronounce you Husband and Wife.

You may kiss your Bride!

Ladies and gentleman, I present to you Mr. & Mrs. _____!!

Ceremony 13 – Recommitment Ceremony

OFFICIANT: Welcome to the recommitment ceremony of {*Groom*} and {*Bride*}.
The following are some excerpts from the Neale Donald Walsch book, <u>Conversations with God, Book One</u>:

> "Most people enter into relationships with an eye toward what they can get out of them, rather than what they can put into them.
> The purpose of relationships is to decide what part of yourself you'd like to see "show up", not what part of another you can capture and hold.
> There can be only one purpose for relationships, and for all of life:
> To be and to decide Who You Really Are.
> It is very romantic to say you were 'nothing' until that 'special other' came along, but it is not true. Worse, it puts an incredible pressure on the other to be all sorts of things he or she is not.
> Not wanting to let you down, they try very hard to be and do these things until they cannot any more. They can no longer

complete your picture of them. They can no longer fill the roles to which they have been assigned. Resentment builds. Anger follows.

Finally, in order to save themselves, and the relationship, these 'special others' begin to reclaim their real selves, acting more in accordance with Who They Really Are. It is about this time that you say, 'They've really changed.'

It is very romantic to say that now that your special other has entered your life, you feel 'complete'. Yet the purpose of relationship is not to have another who might complete you, but to have another with whom you might share your completeness."

The marriage of {Bride} and {Groom} is about being best friends and equal partners in life. Keeping your communication honest and open will allow you to continue to build trust and love that will last a lifetime.

Your happiness begins within each of you, then grows together in love, creating a safe haven for both of you.

A marriage or a recommitment of marriage vows is a bond to be entered into only after considerable thought, reflection, and prayer. As with any part of life, it has its cycles, its ups and its downs. It has its trials and its triumphs. With full understanding of this, do you, {Groom} and {Bride}, stand here today in the presence of your friends and family, to re-sanctify your commitment to one another?

VOWS OF RECOMMITMENT

OFFICIANT: Do you both seek freely to re-enter into this union? {Bride}, will you cause {Groom} pain?
Is that your intent?

{Groom}, will you cause {Bride} pain?
Is that your intent?

Will you both share each other's pain and seek to ease it?

{*Bride*}, will you share {*Groom*}'s laughter?

{*Groom*}, will you share {*Bride*}'s laughter?

Will you both look for the brightness in life and the positive in one another?

{*Bride*} will you burden {*Groom*}?
Is that your intention?

{*Groom*}, will you burden {*Bride*}?
Is that your intention?

Will you share the burdens of one another, so that your spirits will grow in this union?

{*Bride*}, will you share {*Groom*}'s dreams?

{*Groom*}, will you share {*Bride*}'s dreams?

Will you dream together to create new realities and hopes?

{*Bride*}, will you cause {*Groom*} to be angry?
Will that be your intent?

{*Groom*}, will you cause {*Bride*} to be angry?
Will that be your intent?
Will you both take the heat of anger and use it to temper the strength of your union?

The promises made to one another today are the sacred cords that bind you. Either of you may drop these cords, for as always you hold in your own hands the making or breaking of this union. Your lives and spirits are now joined together in a sacred love. Like the stars of the night skies, your love will always be a constant source of light. Like the earth, your love would be a firm foundation on which to grow.

RING EXCHANGE CEREMONY (existing rings are fine)
OFFICIANT: {*Bride*}, please take your ring, place it on {*Groom*}'s finger, and repeat after me:
{*Groom*}, I promise to love you, to protect, nurture and provide for you, to be your best friend and equal partner. My ring is a symbol of the circle of life, and seals my promises to you.

OFFICIANT:{*Groom*}, please take your ring, place it on {*Bride*}'s finger, and repeat after me:
{*Bride*}, I promise to love you, to protect, nurture, and provide for you, to be your best friend and equal partner. My ring is a symbol of the circle of life, and seals my promises to you.

"The Apache Wedding Blessing"
"Now you will feel no rain, for each of you will be shelter for the other. Now you will feel no cold, for each of you will be warmth to the other.
Now there will be no loneliness, for each of you will be companion to the other. Now you are two persons, but there is only one life before you.
May beauty surround you both in the journey ahead, and through the years. May happiness be your companion, and your days together be good and long upon the earth."
{*Groom*} and {*Bride*}, you may now seal your recommitment to one another with a kiss.

Congratulations!

Ceremony 14 – Spiritual Earth Ceremony

OFFICIANT: The greatest thing you'll ever learn is just to love and be loved in return. Welcome family and friends. We have been brought here today to share with {*Bride*} and {*Groom*} in this sacred space as they commit to each other in the union of marriage. Each of you represent something special to this couple and it is an honor to help them celebrate as they embark on a journey of love. On behalf of {*Bride*} and {*Groom*}, I want to thank you for being here.

The dictionary definition of the word "love" means a profound, tender, passionate affection for one another. Some of the key ingredients in the meaning of life can be found in the words of this definition. We must approach life with a passion, we must greet a fellow stranger with affection, we must treat the earth and all living creatures with tenderness; just as we would treat someone we love. To enter into the union of marriage is the most holy of ways we honor the traditions of life. It is designed to be a selfless act of the greatest humility we can express to another human being. {*Bride*} and {*Groom*}, may you fully commitment with not only your hearts and your words today, but by your actions as you move through your lives together. To truly love is the one thing strongest enough to move mountains, and that my friends, is the only responsibility we have in this life time - just to love and be loved in return.

At this time, I would like to ask you to stand and join me in a prayer.

PRAYER: (*everyone stand - alternate, form circle with bridal party*)
We gather here this Night (day) to bind a man and woman in a ritual of love. Let all who stand, be here of their own free will and that you come with peace in your heart. We ask that this sacred space be filled with love and consecrated before God and Goddess and may it be a Guardian and Protection for the work we do on this Night (day). Let

{*Bride*} and {*Groom*} stand here before us and also in the Presence of the Ancient Ones.

> To the East: Be here with us Spirits of the Air. With your breath of life, join the bonds between these two and tie them tightly.

> To the South: Be here with us Beings of Fire. Give their love and passion all your own consuming devotion.

> To the West: Be here with us Beings of Water. Grant these two the deepest of love; richness of body, soul and spirit.

> To the North: Be here with us Spirits of Earth. Let your strength and constancy be theirs for as long as they desire to be together.

OFFICIANT: Blessed God and Goddess, look with joy upon the Union of this man and this woman. Grant them harmony and beauty in their lives and let them always be mindful of their commitment, one to the other. Let their happiness shine as a beacon for all to see. We thank you for your attendance in our Sacred Ceremony and ask for your blessing upon this couple and upon the commitment they are making here on this Night (day).
Namaste.

VOWS
OFFICIANT: Let us return our attention to the {*Bride*} and {*Groom*} and bear witness as they enter into the holy sacrament of marriage by exchanging their vows.

OFFICIANT: {*Bride*}, repeat after me:
{*Groom*}, I stand before you today, in the presence of God and Goddess, our family and friends, to offer you my heart in a journey

filled with unconditional love. I promise from this day forward, to honor you always, to trust you even in times of struggle, and to respect you for all that you are today and all that you will become tomorrow. I no longer walk this world alone, for today, I am honored to become your wife.

OFFICIANT: *{Bride}*, do you take *{Groom}* to be your lawful husband, your faithful partner, to give and to receive, to speak and to listen, to inspire and to respond?

Bride: I do.

OFFICIANT: This is a commitment made in love, kept in faith and eternally made new.

OFFICIANT: *{Groom}*, repeat after me:
{Bride}, I stand before you today, in the presence of God and Goddess, our family and friends, to offer you my heart in a journey filled with unconditional love. I promise from this day forward, to honor you always, to trust you even in times of struggle, and to respect you for all that you are today and all that you will become tomorrow. I no longer walk this world alone, for today, I am honored to become your husband.

OFFICIANT: *{Groom}*, do you take *{Bride}* to be your lawful wife, your faithful partner, to give and to receive, to speak and to listen, to inspire and to respond?
Groom: I do.

OFFICIANT: This is a commitment made in love, kept in faith and eternally made new.

EXCHANGE OF RINGS

OFFICIANT: It was once thought that there was a vein which ran directly from the ring finger of the left hand to the heart, hence the reason tradition would have us wear a wedding ring on the left hand. The circle is a symbol of the sun, the earth and the universe. It is a symbol that represents a union that is meant to last forever and that no matter where you go, you will always return to one another and to your togetherness. {*Bride*} and {*Groom*} have elected to continue this tradition today with an exchange of their own wedding rings. May I have the rings please? As you offer these rings, it is a token of your love and commitment to each other. May these rings be blessed as symbol of your affectionate unity. Your individual lives are now being joined together in one unbroken circle. May these rings symbolize the spirit of love you have for one another.

OFFICIANT: {*Bride*}, repeat after me:
{*Groom*}, I give you this ring as a symbol of my never-ending love. I marry you with this ring, with all that I have and all that I am.

OFFICIANT: {*Groom*}, repeat after me:
{*Bride*}, I give you this ring as a symbol of my never-ending love. I marry you with this ring, with all that I have and all that I am.

CONCLUSION OF CEREMONY
OFFICIANT: Above you are the Stars and below you are the stones. As time passes remember this: like a stone, your love should be firm. Be close, but grant each other freedom to grow. Be understanding and compassionate.
Be supportive and nurturing. Share in each other's dreams. Have patience with each other, for storms may come, but they will quickly go. Be free in giving warmth and affection and never take each other for granted. Let the stars that shine above you be as bright as they are today, for all the days of your life. May peace and love be with you.

Let us now celebrate what the Universe has brought together and so it is, and so it shall be! By the power vested in me, I now pronounce you husband and wife.

You may kiss your Bride!

Ladies and gentlemen, family and friends, it gives me great pleasure to introduce to you for the very first time, Mr. & Mrs. _____!!

7

ঙ৹৻ঙ

Samples of Unity Sand, Earth and Candle Ceremonies

A unity Ceremony is very popular in both traditional and nontraditional wedding ceremonies. There are a variety of unity ceremonies each focusing just a little differently. The unity candle focusing on the light within us all or representing the element of fire. The unity sand ceremonies represent the grains of sand, unable to be separated, symbolizing unity and eternity. Some sand ceremonies are as simple as the Bride and Groom tossing handfuls of sand together into the wind. The unity earth ceremony is unique, as the bride and groom focus on bringing the energy of the earth from the land of their loved ones. It symbolizes the love and support they have from all over the country. All unity ceremonies can be done with a keepsake that symbolizes the new family and their never ending love.

Unity Sand Ceremony 1
OFFICIANT: Today, this relationship is symbolized through the pouring of these two individual containers of sand; one, representing you, {*Bride*} and all that you were, all that you are, and all that you will ever be; and the other,

representing you, {*Groom*}, and all that you were and all that you are, and all that you will ever be. As these two containers of sand are poured into the third container, the individual containers of sand will no longer exist, but will be joined together as one. Just as these grains of sand can never be separated and poured again into the individual containers, so will your marriage be.

Unity Sand Ceremony 2
OFFICIANT: {*Bride*} and {*Groom*}, today you join your separate lives together. The two separate bottles of sand symbolize your separate lives, separate families and separate sets of friends. They represent all that you are and all that you'll ever be as an individual. They also represent your lives before today. As these two containers of sand are poured into the third container, the individual containers of sand will no longer exist, but will be joined together as one. Just as these grains of sand can never be separated and poured again into the individual containers, so will your marriage be.

Unity Sand Ceremony 3
OFFICIANT: Today, {*Bride*} and {*Groom*}, have chosen to commemorate their marriage through the celebration of the Sand Ceremony. This ceremony symbolizes the inseparable union of {*Bride*} and {*Groom*} into a new and eternal marital relationship. {*Bride*} and {*Groom*} will simultaneously pour separate containers of sand into a common vessel. Each grain of sand in their separate containers represents a unique and separate moment, decision, feeling or event that helped shaped {*Bride*} and {*Groom*} into the separate and unique individuals that they are today. As they pour their separate containers of sand into a common vessel, those separate and independent individuals will cease to exist. Instead they will merge into a loving and supportive marital community.

{*Bride*} and {*Groom*}, just as the grains of sand can never be separated into their individual containers again, so will your marriage be.

Unity Sand Ceremony 4 – Vows

OFFICIANT: Please note this empty glass. Glass itself is made from sand, and the sands of time have come together, melting into one piece, to make this vessel. The sands of time should remind us all of our eternal love and our mortality. Today {*Bride*} and {*Groom*} have chosen to represent their love to each other in a special sand ceremony. Please {*Bride*} and {*Groom*}, take your separate glass of sand and alternate the pouring of sand into this joining vessel and united, repeat after me:

You are my love for eternity. I blend with you. My heart is like these grains of sands, merging with yours. I am yours. You are mine. We are together forever like the sand, like the wind. We are one.

Unity Sand Ceremony 5 – Child/Children

OFFICIANT: I'd now like to invite {*Children*} to come up for the Unity Sand ceremony.

Today, this relationship is symbolized through the pouring of this sand, each color representing a member. As each individual's sand is poured into the family's one united container, the individual containers of sand will no longer exist, but will be joined together as one. Just as these grains of sand can never be separated and poured again into the individual containers, so will become the bond with your family.

We begin with a layer of neutral sand which symbolizes that the marriage is grounded. (*This sand is already in the base of the container.*)

Then we layer the individual colors. This symbolizes that the marriage is based on the strength of the individuals. *(Groom pours some of his sand in, followed by Bride pouring about the same amount, and then each Child pours about the same amount.)* And now we combine the color, which symbolizes all these lives joined as one family together forever. *(Everyone pours sand into large vase together so that the colors combine until their jars are empty.)*

Unity Earth Ceremony

OFFICIANT: {*Groom*} and {*Bride*}, you have learned much in your individual lives. Your families brought you life and taught you your first lessons about love. Everyone here with you today has been a part of your individual lives, and has shared your hopes, dreams, triumphs and sufferings. Then you met one another. There is a special way that you are together that is not like the way you have ever been with anyone else. You have a way of sharing with each other, of laughing, and joking together that is unlike with anyone else. As your lives come together in unity, your families will also unite to share in your joy. As a symbol of the blending of two lives, two families and a gathering of friends, you have asked that everyone here bring you dirt from across the miles to combine together to symbolize the blending of Earth and soil that nurtures life. **[Earth will now be combined in the glass container].**

{*Groom*} and {*Bride*}: With this soil, we will plant a plant and watch it grow as we grow old together in love. We thank everyone for being a part of our special union.

Unity Candle Ceremony 1

OFFICIANT: {*Groom*} and {*Bride*} will commemorate their marriage by lighting a Unity Candle *(Bride and groom walk over* *to the candles)*

Light is the essence of our existence. Each one of us possesses an inner glow that represents our hopes, our dreams and aspirations in life.

{*Groom*} and {*Bride*, the two distinct candle flames represent your lives before this day, individual, unique and special. Please take the candle symbolizing your life before today, and together light the center candle to symbolize the union of your individual lives. *(Place the tapers back into their holders—join hands and remain near the candles)* As this new flame burns undivided, so shall your lives now be one. From now on your thoughts will always be for each other rather than just your individual selves. Your plans will be mutual, your joys and sorrows both will be shared alike.

Although you are now entering into a marriage relationship, you do not, however, lose your personal identity. Rather, you will use your special individuality to create and strengthen the relationship of marriage. Therefore all three candles remain glowing. The individual candles represent all that makes each of you the wonderful and unique person the other admires and respects. The Unity candle in the center symbolizes the union of your lives, families, and friends, as well as your shining commitment to each other, and to a lasting and loving marriage. *(Walk back to wedding officiant)*

Unity Candle Ceremony 2
OFFICIANT: {*Groom*} and {*Bride*}, the two separate candles symbolize your separate lives, separate families and separate sets of friends. I ask that each of you take one of the lit candles and that together you light the center candle. The individual candles represent your lives before today. Lighting

the center candle represents that your two lives are now joined to one light, and represents the joining together of your two families and sets of friends to one. *(As couple walks back to officiant, I read the following)*

May the blessing of light,
Be with you always,
Light without and light within.
And may the sun shine
Upon you and warm your heart
Until it glows
Like a great fire
So that others may feel
The warmth of your love
For one another.

Unity Candle Ceremony 3 – Children

OFFICIANT: Each person is unique, and each of us is born with special gifts. Within each of us there is a light that reaches straight to the heavens. And when two people like {*Groom*} and {*Bride*} find each other, their light touches together and a single brighter light is created from their being together. When a family is formed as an extension of this union, the light gets even brighter because of the light that flows from the children as well. The purpose of human love is to awaken love for life. Within each person burns the spark of life, and when people love one another, they make each other more aware of that spark within each other. I'd like to ask each person to take their candle and together light the center candle, symbolizing the new and greater flame of your family, remembering that just as this union is made stronger by your strength as individuals, so are you as individuals made stronger by the strength of this union.

Unity Candle Ceremony 4

OFFICIANT: {*Groom*} and {*Bride*}, the two separate candles symbolize your separate lives, separate families and separate sets of friends. I ask that each of you take one of the lit candles and that together you light the center candle. The individual candles represent your lives before today. Lighting the center candle represents that your two lives are now joined to one light, and represents the joining together of your two families and sets of friends to one. *(As couple walks back to officiant, I read the following)*

"Soft mists embrace two golden flames,
Alone they search the night.
Two souls adrift in dreams of love,
They seek to claim the light.
The path is long from which they came,
But sure they are it's right.
Two flames embrace in dreams of love,
Two Souls – Two Hearts Unite."

Unity Candle Ceremony 5 - Mothers (or parents) light the candles OFFICIANT: *(To guests)* You have been invited today because you are the people—the friends and family-- that are most important to {*Groom*} and {*Bride*}. They want you to share their happiness, and to witness their new beginnings as a family. We are all here today to celebrate this love and commitment. It is appropriate that you, the family and friends are here to participate in this wedding. The ideals, the understanding, and the mutual respect, which these two bring to their marriage have roots in the love, friendship, and guidance, with which you have provided them.

These two outer candles represent the separate families and pasts from which {*Groom*} and {*Bride*} come from. Today these two come together to be joined as one. As a symbol of your blessing, will the mothers please come up and light the outer two candles. *(Mothers light candles.)*

Above you, below you, forever surrounding you, shall be the pledge you make unto each other today. It is the pledge of the truth and purity of your every breath; the constant friendship in your hearts; the passion and fire of your spirits and the deepest love your souls have to give. It is the pledge of all that is within you; the only true pledge that one heart can offer to another. {*Groom*} and {*Bride*}, would you now light the center candle as a symbol of this pledge? *(Couple lights candle.)*

Soft mists embrace two golden flames, Alone they search the night. Two souls adrift in dreams of love, They seek to claim the light. The path is long from which they came, but sure they are it's right. Two flames embrace in dreams of love Two souls- two hearts unite.

8

೮ಾಅ

Wedding Prayers, Blessings & Poems

Opening Prayer

Heavenly Father, _____ and _____ are now about to vow their unending loyalty to each other. We ask you to accept the shared treasure of their life together, which they now create and offer to You. Grant them everything they need, that they may increase in their knowledge of You throughout their life together. In the name of Jesus. Amen.

"To Be One With Each Other" by George Eliot

What greater thing is there for two human souls
than to feel that they are joined together to strengthen
each other in all labor, to minister to each other in all sorrow,
to share with each other in all gladness,
to be one with each other in the
silent unspoken memories?

"An Irish Wedding Blessing"

You are the star of each night,
You are the brightness of every morning,

You are the story of each guest,
You are the report of every land.
No evil shall befall you, on hill nor bank,
In field or valley, on mountain or in glen.
Neither above, nor below, neither in sea,
Nor on shore, in skies above,
Nor in the depths.
You are the kernel of my heart,
You are the face of my sun,
You are the harp of my music,
You are the crown of my company

"Marriage is a Promise of Love"

Marriage is a commitment to life- to the best that two people can find and bring out in each other. It offers opportunities for sharing and growth no other human relationship can equal, a physical and emotional joining that is promised for a lifetime.

Within the circle of its love, marriage encompasses all of life's most important relationships. A wife and a husband are each other's best friend, confidant, lover, teacher, listener, and critic. There may come times when one partner is heartbroken or ailing, and the love of the other may resemble the tender caring of a parent or child.

Marriage deepens and enriches every facet of life. Happiness is fuller, memories are fresher, commitment is stronger, even anger is felt more strongly, and passes away more quickly.

Marriage understands and forgives the mistakes life is unable to avoid. It encourages and nurtures new life, new experiences, and new ways of expressing love through the seasons of life.

When two people pledge to love and care for each other in marriage, they create a spirit unique to themselves, which binds them closer than any spoken or written words. Marriage is a promise, a potential, made in the hearts of two people who love, which takes a lifetime to fulfill.

"Remember" by Steve Goodier

Remember that your presence is a present to the world.
Remember that you are a unique and unrepeatable creation.
Remember that your life can be what you want it to be.
Remember to count your blessings, not your troubles.
Remember that you'll make it through whatever comes along.
Remember that most of the answers you need are within you.
Remember those dreams waiting to be realized.
Remember that decisions are too important to leave to chance.
Remember to always reach for the best that is within you.
Remember that nothing wastes more energy than worry.
Remember that not getting what you want
is sometimes a wonderful stroke of luck.
Remember that the longer you carry a grudge,
the heavier it gets.
Remember not to take things too seriously.
Remember to laugh.
Remember that a little love goes a long way.
Remember that a lot goes forever.
Remember that happiness is more often found in giving
than getting.
Remember that life's treasures are people, not things.
Remember that miracles still happen.

"Blessing for a Marriage" by James Dillet Freeman

May your marriage bring all the exquisite excitements
A marriage should bring,
And may life grant you also patience, tolerance, and understanding.
May you always need one another-
Not so much to fill your emptiness, as to help you to know your
fullness.
A mountain needs a valley to be complete.
The valley does not make the mountain less, but more;
And the valley is more a valley because it has a mountain towering

over it.

So let it be with you and you.

May you need one another, but not out of weakness.

May you want one another, but not out of lack.

May you entice one another, but not compel one another.

May you embrace one another, but not encircle one another.

May you succeed in all important ways with one another,

And not fail in the little graces.

May you look for thing to praise, often say, "I love you!"

And take no notice of small faults.

If you have quarrels that push you apart,

May both of you hope to have good sense enough to take the first
step back.

May you enter into the mystery which is the awareness of

One another's presence -

No more physical than spiritual, warm and near when you are side by
side,

And warm and near when you are in separate rooms or even distant
cities.

May you have happiness, and may you find it making one another
happy.

May you have love, and may you find it loving one another!

Thank you, God,

For Your presence here with us

And Your blessings on this marriage.

Amen

"Namaste" Prayer

This simple word uttered with a gesture of folded hands is among the
finest salutations mankind has ever been able to vocalize. It simply
means: "I honor the place in you, in which the entire Universe dwells.
That place of Love and Light and of Truth and of Peace. When you
are in that place in you and I am in that place in me, We are One."

"Namaste." (*bow*)

Closing Prayer

Join with me as we ask God's blessing on this new couple. Eternal Father, Redeemer, we now turn to you; and as the first act of this couple in their newly formed union, we ask you to protect their home. May they always turn to you for guidance, for strength, for provision and direction. May they glorify you in the choices they make, in the ministries they involve themselves in, and in all that they do. Use them to draw others to yourself, and let them stand as a testimony to the world of your faithfulness. We ask this in Jesus' name, Amen.

"The Apache Wedding Blessing"

Now you will feel no rain, for each of you will be shelter for the other. Now you will feel no cold, for each of you will be warmth to the other.

Now there will be no loneliness, for each of you will be companion to the other. Now you are two persons, but there is only one life before you.

May beauty surround you both in the journey ahead, and through the years. May happiness be your companion, and your days together, be good and long upon the earth.

9

ᏸᎧᏯ

Scripture Passages

1 Corinthians chapter 13: verses 4-7

Love is patient, love is kind. It does not envy, it does not boast, it is not proud.

It is not rude, it is not self-seeking, it is not easily angered, it keeps no record of wrongs.

Love does not delight in evil, but rejoices with the truth.

It always protects, always trusts, always hopes, always preservers.

Ecclesiastes 4:9-12

Two are better than one,

because they have a good return for their labor:

If either of them falls down, .

one can help the other up.

But pity anyone who falls

and has no one to help them up.

Also, if two lie down together, they will keep warm.

But how can one keep warm alone?

Though one may be overpowered,

two can defend themselves.
A cord of three strands is not quickly broken.

Proverbs 30:18-19
There are three things that amaze me—
no, four things that I don't understand:
how an eagle glides through the sky,
how a snake slithers on a rock,
how a ship navigates the ocean,
how a man loves a woman.

1 Corinthians 13:13
And now these three remain: faith, hope and love. But the greatest of
these is love.

10

ಬ⊃ಲ೮

Last Minute Suggestions,

Tips & Reminders

❖ I know I have said this before, but I'm going to repeat myself. Make sure your license is valid in the state you are going to perform the ceremony. Not all states accept the "internet ordinations." The last thing you want to do is perform a wedding ceremony and then find out afterwards you were not legally able to do so and the couple is not legally married. So check with your state to make sure you meet the qualifications.

❖ If the wedding is in a church, make sure you have met the church's requirements for being able to perform a wedding. Depending on the religion and the church you plan on marrying people in, you may have some additional requirements. Make sure you contact that church ahead of time to see if you qualify or if there is something you need to do in order to qualify.

❖ Pay attention to how long or how short the ceremony is. If it is only 10 minutes, you may want to suggest adding a little more to make people feel like there was a reason to show up. Alternatively, if it is too long, people tend to get bored and start checking out. I have found that a 25-30 minute ceremony is about perfect. To get an idea.. read through the entre ceremony slowly, that will give you a basic idea of the amount of time.

❖ What to wear? I wear a black pantsuit or a black business length skirt regardless of the theme or color. If it is in a church, or the couple requests it, I will wear a stole. You can purchase a stole through a church supply catalog or have one made just for you.

❖ Once you are home, make a copy of the signed license for your records and then send it in right away. Send it in for them, as part of your service, so they don't have to worry about it and you know it is done.

❖ You may have noticed that in some ceremonies, I use {*Bride*} & {*Groom*} and in others I use {*Groom*} & {*Bride*}. it is just a matter of their preference. Ask them how they prefer it to be.

❖ I like to have the coupe bring the marriage license to the rehearsal dinner and hand it over to me. That way, in the chaos of the special day, it doesn't get forgotten. You do not want to forget the license either.

❖ I arrive at the venue about an hour to an hour and a half before the wedding is to begin. This way I can check in on my bride, my groom, the family, and get a vibe for the space before everyone arrives.

❖ Each state and church has laws about who can perform weddings and who can't. Do not forget to check that out. Laws are different in every state. Not everyone can do a wedding anywhere. **Be sure you are legal!**

Appendix A

Online Resources

Processional

http://weddings.about.com/od/yourweddingceremony/a/Processional.htm

Marriage Laws

http://www.usmarriagelaws.com/search/united_states/officiants_requirements/index.shtml

http://marriage.about.com/cs/marriagelicenses/a/officiants.htm

Wedding Vows

http://weddings.about.com/cs/{Bride}sand{Groom}s/a/vowwording.htm

Ring Ceremony

http://weddings.about.com/od/weddingvows/a/ringceremony.htm

Unity Sand and Other Unity Ceremonies

http://www.calgaryweddingsource.com/unity_sand_ceremony_wording.html

Love and Marriage Quotes

http://www.abeautifulaffairoftheheart.com/LoveAndMarriageQuotes.html

Appendix B

Citations

APA: How to Conduct a Wedding Ceremony: 7 Steps - wikiHow. (n.d.). Retrieved from http://www.wikihow.com/Conduct-a-Wedding-Ceremony

APA: Vancouver Officiant. (n.d.). Retrieved from http://vancouverofficiant.tumblr.com/

APA: Unity Candle Ceremony Tradition. (n.d.). Retrieved from http://affordabledestinationbeachwedding.com/index.php/wedding-ceremony-traditio ns/item/105-unity-candle-ceremony-tradition

APA: Marriage Poems-Wedding Vows-Love Poems-Bible Verses-Quotes ... (n.d.). Retrieved from https://www.documentsanddesigns.com/verse/marriage_poems.ht m

APA: R Nuptials - Rebecca Zelanin Wedding Officiant | Columbus OH ... (n.d.). Retrieved from http://rnuptials.com/createyourownceremony/unitycandleceremony .html

APA: Wedding Sand Ceremony review | buy, shop with friends, sale ... (n.d.). Retrieved from http://www.kaboodle.com/reviews/wedding-sand-ceremony

APA: Grandma and Grandpa Russell - GrandmaandGrandpa. (n.d.). Retrieved from http://brookecarolinemedcalf.com/GrandmaandGrandpa.html

APA: Letter of Good Standing - Get Ordained and how to become a ... (n.d.). Retrieved from http://www.open-ministry.org/open-ministry-letter-good-standing-p-29.html

APA: Wedding Planning Guide | Bible.org. (n.d.). Retrieved from https://bible.org/article/wedding-planning-guide

APA: Getting Married in Phoenix, Marriage License Fee, AZ. (n.d.). Retrieved from http://www.usmarriagelaws.com/search/united_states/arizona/pho enix/marriage_lice nses/fees.shtml
APA: Vancouver Officiant. (n.d.). Retrieved from http://vancouverofficiant.tumblr.com/
APA: Wedding Vows - Love Poems - Bible Verses - Quotes - Marriage ... (n.d.). Retrieved from https://www.documentsanddesigns.com/verse/cultural_vows.htm

ABOUT THE AUTHOR

Sunny Dawn Johnston is an inspirational speaker, a compassionate spiritual teacher, an internationally acclaimed psychic medium and author of the bestselling book, Invoking the Archangels - A Nine-Step Process to Heal Your Body, Mind and Soul. In 2003, Sunny founded Sunlight Alliance, LLC, a spiritual teaching and healing center in Glendale, Arizona where she teaches classes via online streaming all over the world. Her classes and workshops have been called Intensive, Intimate, and Healing. She truly is a Wayshower for the Unconditional Love that we all strive for. Sunny is on the faculty at OMEGA Institute, The Infinity Foundation and a featured speaker at Celebrate Your Life. She also volunteers her time as a psychic investigator for the international organization FIND ME. This is a nonprofit organization of psychic, investigative, and canine search-and-rescue volunteers, working together to provide leads to law enforcement and families of missing persons and homicide victims.

Sunny lives in the sunshine of the Arizona desert with her husband, Brett, sons, Crew and Arizona, and their two dogs, Pelé and Xena. To learn more about Sunny's work, see videos, and read articles, please go to her website: www.sunnydawnjohnston.com

Additional Books and Products Available by Sunny Dawn Johnston

BOOKS

Invoking the Archangels - A Nine-Step Process to Heal Your Body, Mind and Soul

Invoking the Archangels Workbook - A Nine-Step Process to Heal Your Body, Mind and Soul

No Mistakes - How You Can Change Adversity into Abundance

Living Your Purpose

Find Me

MEDITATION AND TEACHING CD'S

Invoking the Archangels – To Heal Mind, Body & Soul (Meditation CD)

Embracing The Body That Is - A Guide To Loving Yourself

Soul Transitions - A Medium's Guide to the Spirit World

Sunny Dawn Johnston Archangel Michael Meditation

Conversations with Sunny

Prosperity Affirmations CD

Positive Affirmations CD

PRODUCTS

Invoking the Archangels Oracle Card Deck

Invoking the Archangels Candle Set

Invoking the Archangels Wallet Cards

Invoking the Archangels Mouse Pad

Living Your Purpose Affirmation Cards

Sunny Dawn Jewelry - Angel Jewelry for your Soul

Made in the USA
San Bernardino, CA
28 April 2014